GENOCIDE UNDER THE RED SUN

A memoir and warning for the present day

Roostam Sadri

BA Hons, MBA

Published in Australia by Sid Harta Books & Print Pty Ltd,
ABN: 34632585293
23 Stirling Crescent, Glen Waverley, Victoria 3150 Australia
Telephone: +61 3 9560 9920, Facsimile: +61 3 9545 1742
E-mail: author@sidharta.com.au

First published in Australia 2022
This edition published 2023

Photos are credited to the Sadri family collection.

Cover design, typesetting: WorkingType (www.workingtype.com.au)

Note: All the events described in this book are based on true historical facts, most of which can also be derived from the bibliography at the end of the book. If there are any errors or omissions, they are the author's only and nobody else should be blamed or held accountable for them.

Roostam Sadri
Genocide Under the Red Sun
ISBN: 978-1-922958-08-2 (paperback)
978-0-6456941-8-5 (ebook)

Dedication

This book is dedicated to the memory of my late parents — my father Sagit Sadri and my mother Lailya Sadri nee Gabitova — whose determination to enjoy free and happy lives in Australia was realised after nineteen years of struggle with the Chinese Communist Regime.

Acknowledgements

I wish to acknowledge contributions of many generations of historians, scholars and writers, as well as participants, in the events described in this book. Their efforts and sacrifices made over the centuries must be remembered by posterity.

Disclaimer

I wish to make a disclaimer that if there are any omissions as well as any errors made in this book, they are all mine alone and nobody else should be held responsible for them.

Contents

Introduction

Winston Churchill once said, *"Those that fail to learn from history are doomed to repeat it."*

In recent years, I have been troubled by the news of human rights abuses that have been pouring out of China. Having grown up in what could be called the most brutal period of the Chinese communist regime, I know firsthand the suffering that those in power will inflict on the powerless.

It is unfathomable that the regime that my family escaped from and once thought a relic has risen like a phoenix to take centre stage as a world power. It has been enslaving the ethnic minorities of East Turkestan (Xinjiang), Tibet and Inner Mongolia as a source of cost-free labour, confining them to a vast network of so-called 'vocational skills education centres', prevalent especially throughout Xinjiang to detain and inflict atrocities on Uighurs as well as on other Muslim minorities living there.

I have written this book to first share my story so that you may know firsthand the realities of life under Chairman Mao's regime proclaimed by his stooges to be the 'Red Sun' of China. I then hope to educate you on the neglected history of the Tatar nation, most of them now living further to the north-west from China. Finally, I wish to give you the truth about

China as I witnessed myself when I was living there, as well as told to me by those who have reached out from within in recent times.

I have also decided to begin this book with a chapter titled 'History and Foundations of Islam', which was written by me in Russian in the year 1990 at the request of the then Minister of Education of the Russian Federation, the Hon Mr Saburov, who, during his short tenure as the Minister, wanted to reform the Russian high school curriculum by producing new textbooks and also to include a textbook on the history of religions for the Russian high schools. Mr Saburov, however, lost his job when the Soviet Union disintegrated shortly afterwards, before his ideas about reforms and new textbooks for Russian schools were implemented. This year marks the 1,100th anniversary of the voluntary adoption of Islam in the year 922 by the Tatar people of the Kingdom of Bulgar, so this writing has now acquired a special significance for interested readers, even if it ended up never getting published in Russia in 1990.

1

History and Foundations of Islam

Foreword

Islam occupies a special place among the great religions of the world not only because the number of its adherents globally now exceeds more than one billion people, but also due to its importance as a simple and easily understood religion. Islam forms the basis of the world outlook and everyday behaviour for Muslims, or adherents to Allah, in Arabic. All believers in Islam must adhere to the one and only God, the Creator of the Universe and all the living creatures inhabiting it. Prophet Muhammed—Peace Be Upon Him (PBUH)—is recognised as the Messenger of God who accomplished the works of His predecessors such as Jesus, Moses and Abraham, as well as all other prophets starting with Adam as the First Prophet on the Planet Earth, according to the Holy Koran. As a monotheistic religion, Islam shares many common religious concepts with Christianity and Judaism, which preceded Islam. It reveres Jesus Christ as the Messenger of God—the Prophet—but not as the Son of God. The central tenet of Islam declares, 'God is One and Muhammed is the Messenger of God'. As mentioned earlier, Islam also recognises Jesus, Moses, Abraham as well as all other prophets mentioned in the Bible as well as in the Torah, starting with Adam. According to the Holy Koran, they were all sent to deliver God's message to mankind. Every person who utters this phrase, believing in it, becomes a Muslim regardless of gender, race or nationality. In order to strengthen their faith, all believers then should accept the existence of God without a beginning or end, without any equals, without dependence on anything or anybody, the uniqueness of God Almighty, the All-Knowing, All-Seeing, All-Hearing God that extends His will into everything around us. Islam demands absolute honesty, truthfulness and compassion towards everybody else regardless of their origins and religion. It also demands ongoing diligence in everyday life from its adherents. The Holy Book of Islam is the Koran comprised of 114 suras, or chapters. Muslims believe that the Holy Koran is God's revelation to Prophet Muhammed conveyed by Archangel Gabriel over two decades starting when he was forty years of age, or in the year 610 AD and ending shortly before his death in 632 AD. To honour Prophet Muhammed, it is customary for Muslims to add the phrase 'Peace Be Upon Him' after his name.

Emergence of Islam in Arabia

The emergence and rapid expansion of Islam on the Arabian Peninsula is closely linked to the biography of the Prophet Muhammed PBUH. Prophet Muhammed PBUH was born in the year 570 AD to the family of Abdullah from Hashim Clan of the Koreishy tribe. His father passed away before the boy's birth. His mother, Amina, also passed away when young Muhammed was only six years old. The orphan was adopted by his grandfather, Abdul Muttallib, who loved him very much, but he also passed away after Muhammed turned eight years old. His uncle, Abu Talib, took him in, where he had to look after his uncle's sheep and help with everyday household chores. When Muhammed turned twelve years old, his uncle took him on a trip to Syria, where, in the city of Basra, they met with a holy Christian monk by the name of Bahira, who predicted a great future for Muhammed and told his uncle to protect him in every possible way. When Muhammed turned twenty-four years of age, he started working for a wealthy widow in Mecca by the name of Hadicha Bint Huvaylid. At the age of twenty-five, Muhammed married her by accepting her proposal of marriage. Their marriage was a happy one. They succeeded in bearing six children—two boys and four girls. Unfortunately, only two girls survived to grow up to adulthood—the famously beautiful Rokya and Fatima—whose offspring continued the Prophet's lineage. Prophet Muhammed PBUH loved to retreat sometimes into a cave near Mecca, which was called 'Cave

Hara', in order to meditate and pray. Once, when he turned forty years of age, he was meditating in the cave when he saw a vision of Archangel Gabriel in front of him, conveying to him the first sura, or chapter, of the Holy Koran. Archangel Gabriel told him to spread God's revelation, as he was chosen to become the last Prophet on Earth to complete the work of his predecessor prophets. God's revelation expressed the main message of Islam about faith in the One and Only God, faith in God's messengers beginning with Prophet Adam and ending with Prophets Jesus and Muhammed, and belief in the Day of Judgement. Then Muhammed learned about the main rituals of Islam prior to offering prayers, such as how to wash your hands and face, feet, mouth and nose. Then about the order of reading the main prayers of Islam and the physical order of body movements during the conduct of prayer.

The main tenets of Islam demand friendliness and honesty to everyone, reverence towards parents and to the next of kin, and friendliness to neighbours and everybody else as well. Islam also demands impeccable honesty, truthfulness, compassion and kindness between all people, considering hard work, as well as exercising temperance in eating habits and other physical bodily requirements, as positive virtues. The first sura, or chapter of the Koran, declares, 'In the name of Allah, the Most Beneficent, the Most Merciful, Praise be to Allah, the Cherisher and Sustainer of the worlds, Most Gracious, Most Merciful, Master of the Day of Judgement. You do we worship, and Your aid we seek. Show us the straight way, the way of those on whom You bestowed Your way, not the way of those who earned Your anger, nor of those who went astray.'

The First Muslims

Idolatry, drunkenness and gambling were rife in Arabia at the end of the sixth century AD. Arabs in those days did not adhere to high moral standards, even stooping sometimes to the lowly habit of burying their newborn daughters alive in the sand out of fear that they would not be able to feed them, whereas newborn boys were regarded as potential future working hands in the household. In such conditions, Prophet Muhammed assumed the very difficult task of turning such a lowly, ignorant crowd into civilised people with high moral standards demanded by Islam. By the time the Prophet commenced his lofty mission, many people around him already respected him for his truthfulness and honesty. When he conveyed his thoughts to his wife, Hadicha, she immediately converted to Islam, thus becoming the first Muslim. Then the other members of the Prophet's family—his nephew, Ali Ibn Abu Talib; his former slave, Zaid Ibn Harita, whom the Prophet adopted as his son; and close friend, Abu Bakr—also converted to Islam. Prophet Muhammed continued to secretly preach the Islamic faith, so the number of his adherents kept increasing. These first adherents of Islam, who converted and lived alongside Prophet Muhammed, were called his sahaba, or comrades, as they were his friends who shared with him all his difficulties in life.

Leaders of Koreishy Tribe and their animosity towards the Prophet

Leaders of the Koreishy tribe in Mecca, who owned the city of Mecca and used its idolatry temples as lucrative business ventures, became upset with the new religion of Islam, as they perceived it as a threat to their well-being. Mecca was the centre of all idolatry-adhering Arabs of that time, benefitting the Meccan leadership of the time as a centre of trade as well as a centre of religious tourism for Arabia. Once, Prophet Muhammed invited all Meccan leaders to his house to be his guests. He asked them, 'Would you believe me if I told you that the enemies are approaching us from behind these mountains?' They replied, 'Yes, we believe you, as you never ever lied to us before.' The Prophet then told them, 'You must stop worshipping idols, as God's punishment shall befall you if you continue worshipping idols.' All the leaders of the Koreishy tribe present, including the uncle of the Prophet, Abu Lahab, got very angry at Prophet Muhammed and left his house. Followers of Prophet Muhammed became the target of their attacks. Once Prophet Muhammed was nearly killed by Abu Jahil, who managed to throw a rope over his neck and started to suffocate him. The Prophet was saved by Abu Bakr, who saw what was happening. Many slaves, who belonged to the idol worshippers of Mecca, also started to adopt Islam as slavery was forbidden in Islam according to the teachings of Prophet Muhammed that all people were equal in Islam. The owners of these slaves often punished them and even tortured them to force them to denounce Islam. Many of these slaves were then purchased by Abu Bakr using Prophet Muhammed's money and were liberated from slavery. One of them was Bilal Ibn Rabah, a black slave from Abyssinia, who belonged to a rich man named Umaya Ibn Halaf. Umaya once threw Bilal on hot sand and put heavy stones all over him to force him to denounce Islam. Abu Bakr bought Bilal, who was very weakened by the torture, and immediately released him from slavery. Subsequently, Bilal ended up becoming one of the military chiefs close to Prophet Muhammed. Gradually, converts to Islam in Mecca increased to the point that, in desperation, the leaders of the Koreishy tribe of Mecca offered him half their wealth and the post of being their king if he stopped spreading Islam in Mecca and left their idols alone. They were not able to kill Prophet Muhammed, as the tribal rules of blood retribution would have befallen them from two powerful clans of Mecca—Banu Hashim and Banul Muttalib—that protected Prophet Muhammed as he was related to both groups. These two clans would have lost their honour among the other tribal groups of Arabia if they failed to protect Prophet Muhammed. According to the Arab customs of the time, Abu Talib, the uncle of Prophet Muhammed, was the leader of these two powerful clans. He loved his nephew, so the influence and power of these two clans protected Prophet Muhammed from any serious attempts on his life while his uncle was still alive. Hijra, the Koreishy tribesmen of Mecca, even attempted to boycott the Banu Hashim and Banu Muttalib clans of Prophet Muhammed over three years, by trying to enforce economic and political blockades. They were excluded from trading with other Koreishy tribesmen. Nothing was sold to them or purchased from them. Nobody was supposed to marry members of those two clans. All these efforts, however, turned out to be useless, as the numbers of converts to Islam kept gradually increasing even beyond Mecca. Islam kept spreading into such cities as Yathrib (Medina), and even into Abyssinia because some Muslims decided to leave Mecca to avoid persecution there and ended up settling into new communities, where many people converted to Islam as well. When the boycott of the Prophet's relatives ended after three years due to its failure, everything went back to normal for them. But soon two very sad events took place for Prophet Muhammed: in 619 AD he lost his beloved wife, Hadicha, as well as his uncle, Abu Talib, in the same month. The passing of Abu Talib enabled the enemies of Prophet Muhammed to resume their hostilities. Prophet Muhammed decided to go to the city of Taif located higher up in the hills above Mecca by more than one hundred kilometres. The idol-worshipping inhabitants of Taif, however, decided to chase him out of Taif by ordering their slaves and children to throw stones at him, despite the fact that they were not that friendly to the Koreishy tribesmen of Mecca. The inhabitants of Yathrib (Medina), which was located some 445 km to the north-west of Mecca, once they learned about Prophet Muhammed's difficulties, decided to invite him to come to them. A group of them from Yathrib came to Mecca one year after the sad events for Prophet Muhammed. He met with six of them, who converted to Islam after talking to Prophet Muhammed, and promised to persuade all their tribesmen in Yathrib to convert to Islam as well. During the following two years the number of Muslims in Yathrib grew to the point where 76 of them, including two women, came to Mecca to ask him to relocate to Yathrib with all of his followers to become their leader. Yathrib, known as Medina now, was then a flourishing oasis with date palm plantations, a proper irrigation system and plentiful grain-growing fields as well as grape plantations. Its inhabitants, nonetheless, often suffered from ongoing blood feuds and killings, which went on for more than 120 years. Islam was ending blood feuds among various clans as it strictly forbade blood-feud killings and robberies. Teachings of Islam about unity, friendship and equality among all people appealed to all inhabitants of Medina. Prophet Muhammed decided to accept their invitation and ordered all of his followers to start relocating to Medina. He decided to remain in Mecca until most of his followers managed to relocate to Medina. When only Ali, Abu Bakr and some others who were either sick or too old and weak to survive the relocation trip remained in Mecca, the Prophet decided to move as well. His enemies found out about it and decided to kill him. So, as to avoid blood revenge from the Prophet's relatives and followers, a group of young men were told to stalk him near his house at night and attack all at once when he emerged from his house. Prophet Muhammed waited until late at night and then started reading verses from the Holy Koran to put to sleep his enemies outside who were still stalking him. When they all fell asleep, he quietly left his house, together with Abu Bakr, and hid in the cave in the mountains. In the morning, all his angry enemies who had been stalking him could not understand why they had fallen asleep. A big reward was announced for his capture. All those who wanted to collect the reward rushed to search for him. Very soon a group of them located the cave where Prophet Muhammed and Abu Bakr were hiding. By that time, a spider had spun its web at the entrance to the cave and a wild pigeon had built its nest there. As experienced hunters, those who were looking for the Prophet decided at once that there was nobody in the cave upon seeing the spider web and the wild pigeon's nest, so they went away looking elsewhere further on. After spending three days and nights in this cave, Prophet Muhammed and Abu Bakr resumed their journey to Medina. At last, after ten days and nights of a difficult trip on foot over the hot sands of the desert, they arrived at Medina to be met and eagerly welcomed by its inhabitants. Thus began a new era in Muslim history. This trip to Yathrib, or Medina, from Mecca, which began on

10 September 622 AD, is known in the history of Islam as Hijra, or migration. That is when the Muslim lunar calendar started. From then on, Yathrib was called Madinat Al-Nabi, or in other words, the city of the Prophet—Medina.

The Muslim State in Medina

Before the arrival of the Prophet Muhammed in Medina, there were several Arab and Jewish tribes living there, who were often hostile to one another. After the arrival of Prophet Muhammed and his followers into Medina from Mecca and the voluntary conversion of most of its inhabitants into Islam, the overall situation there improved dramatically. Inter-tribal bloodshed was stopped and all the inhabitants of Medina, including the Jewish people, were very happy with the authority of Prophet Muhammed as the head of the Medina community. Many inhabitants of Medina offered part of their properties to newcomers from Mecca, as they were forced to leave most of their belongings and livestock behind, which were then confiscated by the heathens of the Koreishy tribe. Prophet Muhammed at the same time decided to purchase a plot of land and build a mosque on it. All Muslims of Medina helped him to build the mosque. Prophet Muhammed built a small house for himself right next to the mosque with a direct entrance from his house into the mosque. All visitors to

Prophet Muhammed were received by him inside the mosque, which became the spiritual centre of all the Muslims of Medina. All matters relevant to the Muslim community of Medina were discussed in the mosque and all decisions were made there as well. All new converts to Islam learned their prayers and the rules of Islam inside the mosque. The Prophet led the prayers and conducted sermons in the mosque. This mosque is now regarded as the second most important holy place in Islam after the mosque Al-Haram with Kaaba in Mecca, the third holy mosque being Al-Aksa in Jerusalem. These three mosques underwent many reconstructions since the time of the Prophet, getting bigger and more beautiful each time. After the arrival of Prophet Muhammed into Medina, it became a peaceful and prosperous place to live. The inhabitants of Medina, including the Jews, were able to mix with one another peacefully and conduct their religious rites without fearing for their safety or interference from others. The increasing well-being and importance of the Medina community in Arabia worried the Koreishy idol worshippers of Mecca. They felt threatened by the increasing importance of Medina as the centre of Islam, which was diminishing the importance of Mecca as the centre of idol worshippers of Arabia. So, they started to encourage idol-worshipping Bedawi tribesmen to plunder and steal the properties and livestock of the Muslims of Medina. Prophet Muhammed had no choice but to allow his Muslim followers to seize caravans of the Koreishy heathens from Mecca to compensate for the losses inflicted on them by the Koreishy both in Mecca and subsequently in Medina. So, both sides started to prepare for an inevitable military confrontation.

Battle of Badr

Many Muslims, who relocated from Mecca to Medina, lost most of their properties to the heathens of Mecca. Prophet Muhammed decided to punish the heathen Koreishy Meccans by seizing their caravan, richly loaded with goods being transported from Syria to Mecca past Medina by Abu Sufian, one of the wealthy men of Mecca. Prophet Muhammed led 313 fighters to the well called Badr, where the caravan was expected to stop for watering their camels. Abu Sufian somehow learned about the intention to seize the Meccan goods being transported by the caravan from Syria and called enforcements from Mecca to protect the caravan. At the same time, he changed his route and led the caravan away from danger and into Mecca by an alternative route. Once the Meccan fighters learned about the safe passage of the caravan to Mecca, a small number of them decided to avoid fighting with Prophet Muhammed's troops and returned to Mecca. Their leader, Abu Jahil, however, insisted on attacking and finishing off the Muslim contingent from Medina. Prophet Muhammed responded by ordering his men to bury all wells except one, and put his 313 soldiers in front of this single well. Although the Meccan troops had more than one thousand soldiers with more than two hundred horses and camels, they were all very thirsty. To get to the well they had to fight their way there. Prophet Muhammed's soldiers had many skilful archers among them. He also lined up his soldiers in such a way that the attackers had sunlight against their eyes. The Meccan troops panicked in the ensuing battle when Prophet Muhammed's archers killed eleven leaders of the attackers, including two chiefs—Abu Jahil and Utb Ibn Rabig. More than fifty Meccan soldiers were killed and more than seventy were taken hostage. The Muslims also captured more than 150 camels, ten horses and a large number of arms, losing only some fifteen soldiers. The Battle of Badr in 624 AD is a memorable event in the history of Islam. The victory of Muslims in this battle not only guaranteed their future strength, but also made all the Arab idol worshippers recognise the fact that the Muslims became a real political and military force to be respected in the future. All the trophies and animals seized, as well as the ransom paid for the seventy captured Koreishys, strengthened the financial well-being of the Muslims, especially those who relocated from Mecca to Medina. Prophet Muhammed's authority also grew considerably as a result of this victory. The idol-worshipping Meccans finally understood that their lucrative trade with Syria was ending.

Battle of Uhud Hill

The Meccan losses at the Badr well were so significant that they became angry and started to get ready for another attack on Medina. This time they gathered all their forces as well as money and weaponry. They succeeded in mobilising close to three thousand men, two hundred of them on horseback and seven hundred wearing heavy armour. In line with the habits of the Bedawy nomads of Arabia at the time, a dozen or so well-off dames of Mecca also decided to take part in the attack on Medina under the command of Abu Sufian's wife, Hind, who had lost her father, one of her sons, her brother and her uncle during the battle of the Badr well. She took an oath that she would not sleep with her husband until she took revenge on Muslims for the deaths of her family members. This Meccan army arrived at Uhud Hill, located some four or five kilometres from the centre of the oasis Medina after a ten-day march from the west. The Meccans released their horses and camels to graze on the crops of the inhabitants of Medina, who helplessly watched from behind the city walls, where they were hiding from the attackers. On Friday 22nd March 625 AD the Muslims of Medina gathered for a military meeting. One part of them wanted just to protect themselves behind the city walls but others, whose crops and palm plantations were being destroyed by the attackers, demanded that they should start immediate military action. After the Friday lunchtime prayers, they raised the issue again. Prophet Muhammed retreated into his room and shortly afterwards emerged wearing heavy armour. Some of the hotheads came to their senses and stated that they would follow any decision made by the Prophet. He then told those who gathered around him that it was too late to hesitate. Close to one thousand fighters answered his call to arms, but they had only two horses and close to one hundred pieces of heavy armour. The Jews of Medina decided not to participate in the battle, claiming that their day of Sabbath was approaching, when they were not supposed to fight. As they began marching towards Uhud Hill, Prophet Muhammed sent back all of the young, inexperienced boys who joined the march. One of the Medina chieftains, Ibn Ubay, also decided to turn back with three hundred of his followers. By Friday nightfall, only some seven hundred men remained with Prophet Muhammed. On the morning of Saturday 23 March 625 AD, Prophet Muhammed's men took positions on the steep hillside of Uhud, where the Meccan horsemen could not attack them. Once the battle started, it appeared that better-disciplined and skilled Muslim archers were once again defeating the attacking enemy. But the archers, who were ordered to remain on Uhud Hill and prevent the enemy's horsemen from attacking the Muslim fighters from the rear, decided that the battle was won and rushed downhill to collect the trophies, leaving the rear of the Muslim fighters defenceless. The Meccan cavalry hiding on the side of the hill took advantage of this mistake and attacked, creating panic among the Muslim fighters. Some fifteen of them gathered around Prophet Muhammed and managed to retreat up Uhud hill. Prophet Muhammed, who took part in the battle, was slightly wounded. His uncle, Hamza, was badly wounded by the spear of an Abyssinian slave of one of the Meccans, who was promised freedom for taking part in the battle. Hind—wife of Abu Sufian—cut out the liver of Hamza, who was still alive, and enjoyed eating it. By nightfall, the Muslims had lost some seventy men. The rest of them either managed to escape back to Medina or hid on the side of Uhud Hill. Almost all of the Meccans' horses were hit by the archers but otherwise their victory on the battlefield was complete. The Meccans decided to return to Mecca, as they succeeded in inflicting payback for their defeat at Badr.

Prophet Undertakes Pilgrimage to Mecca

Despite the defeat at Uhud Hill, the Muslims of Medina continued to strengthen their influence all over Arabia. The Meccan caravans were not able to travel unimpeded to Syria past Medina. Abu Sufian once again led the Meccans by gathering an army of ten thousand fighters and at the end of March 627 AD attempted to attack Medina. Prophet Muhammed found out about it beforehand and assembled close to three thousand fighters to strengthen the defences of Medina. As Medina was covered by hillsides, except in the north, he decided to get a deep trench dug across it. This was an unusual novelty for the Arabs at the time. The two opposing sides gathered across the trench facing one another and after three weeks of mutual insults and minor skirmishes across the trench, hungry Meccans decided to lift the siege and return home to Mecca. This was a big victory for Prophet Muhammed. All of Arabia understood that if a ten-thousand-strong Meccan army could not do anything against him, then the other tribes should not even think about attacking Medina. The Meccans gradually started to comprehend the meaning of Prophet Muhammed's teachings and two of their most talented military leaders—Halid Ibn Al Walid and Amr Ibn Al-As—decided to convert to Islam and support Prophet Muhammed. In March 628 AD, Prophet Muhammed decided to conduct a pilgrimage, or Haj, to Mecca. Leading two thousand men armed only with swords, he stopped in the Hudaibiya Valley to spend the night there en route to Mecca. Worried Meccans decided to negotiate with Prophet Muhammed and enter into a peace treaty with him. This was a big diplomatic victory for the Muslims. This meant that the Meccans not only recognised Islam as a legitimate religion, but also agreed to allow the Muslims to conduct annual pilgrimages to the Holy Kaaba in the centre of Mecca once a year. Muslims began to gather rapid strength all over the Arabian Peninsula. The Bedawy nomads began to convert to Islam *en masse*. The Meccans finally understood that they were wrong in opposing Prophet Muhammed and his teachings of Islam in the first place, therefore denying themselves a golden opportunity to strengthen Mecca's influence all over the Arabian Peninsula. One year after concluding the Hudaibiya treaty, Prophet Muhammed conducted a pilgrimage to Mecca leading more than two thousand pilgrims. The Meccans were impressed by the discipline and piousness of the Muslims. Thus, the Meccans themselves became ready to convert to Islam as well.

Takeover of Mecca and Triumph of Islam

The Hudaibiya Treaty was violated by the allies of the Meccans from the Banu Bakr tribe at the end of the year 629 AD, when they killed several allies of Medina from the Huzaya tribe. Prophet Muhammed immediately started to get ready to take over Mecca. On 1 January 630 AD, he led a ten-thousand-strong army towards Mecca. All other Bedawy nomads and even many Meccans themselves also started to join his army en route to Mecca. Abu Sufian, whose daughter, Umm Habiba, by then was already married to Prophet Muhammed, came to him begging for peace. The Prophet promised that he would never touch anybody who surrendered without a fight, and that all their houses and properties would be safe for them. Only a few fanatical Meccans attempted to fight back and were immediately either killed or chased away by the Muslim fighters. Prophet Muhammed declared full amnesty to all Meccans except for three of four especially notorious individuals, who had behaved outrageously in the past. All the idols were thrown out of Kaaba and Prophet Muhammed conducted a seven-circle ritual around Kaaba. After that the Meccans passed Prophet Muhammed sitting by the Safa Rock in a long column, swearing allegiance to him in the process. After the takeover of Mecca by the Muslim forces, Mecca became the holy city to all Muslims and the centre of pilgrimage. The Koreishy tribe became one of the most eager proponents of Islam in Arabia instead of being its oppressors as in the past. By the year 631 AD, almost all of the inhabitants of the Arabian Peninsula embraced Islam. At the beginning of the year 632 AD, Prophet Muhammed undertook a solemn pilgrimage to Mecca where he made a sincere speech, announcing that he counted his prophetic mission as accomplished and so he farewelled all those present. After returning to Medina, he fell ill. Feeling that he was approaching the end of his life, he distributed a substantial part of his belongings to the poor and orphans. The Prophet spent several of the last days of his life half-conscious. On the morning of 7th June, he felt better. He got up and went to the mosque. After his last prayers he touchingly expressed his farewell to all those present, after which, having returned home, he gave his last messages to his wives, relatives and close associates. On 8th June 632 AD, Prophet Muhammed passed away.

Islam After Prophet Muhammed

After the death of Prophet Muhammed, the role of the political and spiritual leader of the Muslims was inherited by halifs, or deputies of the prophet, who undertook all the functions of the prophet except for his prophetic messages. During the decade that followed under the leadership of Halif Omar, who died in 644 AD, the Muslims took control of Egypt, Palestine, Syria, Mesopotamia and Iran, having occupied Damascus in 635 AD, Jerusalem in 640 AD, Cairo in 641 AD, Alexandria in 642 AD and Isfahan in 643 AD. Under Halif Usman, who ruled from 644 AD until his death in 656 AD, the Arab empire stretched from Tripoli, Libya, in the west, to the Caucasian Mountains in the north and to the Himalayas in the east. Ali, who was both a cousin as well as a son-in-law to Prophet Muhammed, ruled the Muslim Empire from Usman's death in 656 until 661 AD. After Ali's death in 661 AD, the Muslims split into two religious factions. The majority became known as the Sunnis, or the followers of mainstream Islam, during the Omayyad Dynasty, which ruled from 661 to 750 AD. Followers of Ali became known as the Shiites, who retained loyalty to Ali. Ali was murdered by the followers of the Omayyads in the year 661. The Omayyads took over most of Spain in 711 AD even spreading out to considerable parts of India. Although the Omayyads did not succeed in taking over France because of their defeat in the year 732, the Arabs remained in Spain for seven-and-a-half centuries. The Omayyad Empire in the east spread across the Aral Sea to the banks of Amu Darya River, including considerable parts of Central Asia. Islam flourished under the Omayyads, as they supported scientists, the medical profession, poets and artists, thus turning the Arab East into the world centre of the scientific knowledge and culture of the times. The Abbasid Dynasty took over from the Omayyads in the year 750 AD and ruled for five centuries until 1258 AD, having established their capital city in Baghdad. During that period, Islam spread to the Kingdom of Great Bulgar on the banks of the Edel (Volga) River in the north, known as Tatarstan and Bashkortostan today. The Abbasids, however, gradually lost control over the enormous Muslim territories spreading from Spain into the borders of India and China, from where a number of Muslim dynasties emerged. The Abbasids themselves remained only in Iraq. In Muslim Spain, the Spanish Omayyads continued to rule from the year 756 until 1031 AD, when they were replaced by Al-Moravids and Al-Mohads from North Africa. Catholic kings of Spain, however, managed to gradually squeeze them out of Spain. After the fall of Grenada in 1492 AD, surviving Muslims and the Jews were expelled from Spain by the victorious Christian troops. The title of 'halif' was taken over by the Ottoman Turks in the fourteenth century, who took over the Balkans and gradually expanded their rule to Vienna in the west as well as beyond Crimea in the north over the two decades that followed. The descendants of Babur Shah from Central Asia created the Great Mughal Empire by taking over almost the entire Indian sub-continent and ruling there from 1526 until 1858 AD, when the last Mughal Emperor was dislodged by the British. These regions of the world, where the majority of the population is Muslim, are sometimes called Dar-Ul-Islam in Arabic, or House of Islam in English. Islam has been spreading peacefully all over the world since the times of theAbbasids. In modern times, the vitality and philosophy of Islam are especially evident in various regions of Asia and Africa, where Islam continues to spread among the populations living there.

The Foundations of Islam

Islam dictates to its adherents five main tenets known as the five basics of Islam. The first one is known as 'Shahada' in Arabic, or the statement that 'God (Allah) is one and Muhammed is the Prophet of God'. This statement, when uttered and believed in, turns any person into a Muslim. The word 'Allah' in Arabic means 'God' and is uttered by both Muslim as well as Christian Arabs with the same meaning. The second tenet of Islam is 'Salat' in Arabic, or 'prayer' in English, which should be done five times a day: at dawn, at midday, towards the end of a working day, at sunset, and finally at night. The third tenet of Islam is the 'giving of alms to the needy'. Every Muslim believer must donate one-tenth of his or her income to the needy. In the modern world this requirement is implemented in almost all Muslim countries by the system of taxation. If a Muslim decides to add a donation in addition to the taxes paid, that is always encouraged. The fourth tenet of Islam is to 'observe fasting during the lunar month of Ramazan', when one should not eat or drink during daylight hours and should abstain from other bodily urges. Finally, the fifth tenet of Islam is to 'undertake a pilgrimage to Mecca once in a lifetime', if the person is able to afford it financially, during Eid-Ul-Adha, or during celebrations of the Feast of Sacrifice, which is usually conducted seventy days after the end of the month of Ramazan. These five tenets of Islam are somewhat different among the Sunnis and the Shiites. The Sunnis have four schools of rites: Shafi, Hanafi, Maliki and Hanbali. The Muslims of Russia mostly observe the Hanafi school of rites. These four schools of rites differ very little in terms of the conduct of prayer, which consists of mental meditation during utterance, as well as performing certain bodily movements like gymnastics by doing 'Rukuh', or bending to the ground and touching it with elbows and foreheads in certain prescribed ways, called 'Sajda'. Fasting during the month of Ramazan and the timing of the pilgrimage to Mecca, or Haj, depends on the lunar calendar, which lasts 354 days in any given year, or twelve rotations of the moon around Earth. This results in the lunar year of Muslims lasting eleven days shorter than the solar, or calendar, year. This means that all Muslim holidays and observance of fasting rotate throughout the seasons a full circle every thirty-three years, thus experiencing them during all four seasons. The Muslim calendar starts from the year of 'Hijra', that is, from September

622 AD, when Prophet Muhammed migrated from Mecca to Medina. The Holy Koran strictly forbids for all Muslims the consumption of alcohol, narcotic drugs, pig meat as well as the meat of scavenger animals or dead animals. Muslims are forbidden to gamble or charge excessive interest on loans. There is also the practice of celebrating at naming ceremonies of girls and boys, and the practice of undertaking the circumcision of boys for hygienic reasons. There are also certain burial rituals when prayers for the dead are offered before the dead bodies are washed and wrapped in clean cotton materials prior to burying them in the ground. Both women and men are always regarded as equal in Islam. They are all expected to know the basics of Islam and observe them in everyday life. Islamic men, in addition to that, are also deemed responsible for the upkeep of women and children in their care. The Holy Koran also prescribes that all men and women dress modestly, but does not stipulate that the women wrap themselves up from head to toe, as practised in some culturally backward Arab countries.

Philosophical Teachings in Islam

The mainstream proponents of Islam observe the traditional teachings of Prophet Muhammed stipulated in the 'hadis', or sayings of the prophet in his lifetime. The name 'Sunni

Muslims' is derived from the word Sunna, or the teachings of the Prophet Muhammed observed by him. Some Muslims, however, chose to stay outside the mainstream Sunni Islam. The biggest sect is the Shiya Muslims, who adhere to 'Shiat Ali', or the party of Ali, who was the cousin as well as the son-in-law of Prophet Muhammed, married to his daughter Fatima. Ali was the fourth 'halif' after the death of Prophet Muhammed and was regarded as the most legitimate successor to Prophet Muhammed in contrast to the Omayyads, the offspring of Moavvya, the son of Abu Sufyan. The Shiya Muslims now live predominantly in Iran and Tajikistan, as well as in parts of Iraq and Azerbaijan. The Sunni school of theology believes that the common consensus of religious scholars is sufficient to resolve ongoing religious issues. The Shiyas, on the other hand, believe that one able Imam, or leader, should lead the masses of believers of each generation. Only in the absence of such a leader should a temporary group of theologians lead the believers. The Shiya Muslims, therefore, developed their own school of theology, interpretations of the Holy Koran, their own judicial system, and prayer rituals of their own, different from the Sunnis. They also practise self-immolation during the month of Muharram, when they conduct mass processions commemorating the martyrdom of the sons of Ali—Hassan and Hussain—by beating their backs with chains while howling, 'Ya Hassan, Ya Hussain'. Sunni Muslims frown at such emotional self-immolation practices as alien to the spirit of Islam. One of the interesting schools of thought in Islam is Sufism. The Sunni's Islam does not deploy music when conducting prayers and religious festivities. The Sufis, on the other hand, widely use music, drums and dancing during the conduct of their religious rituals. The Sufis propagate an ascetic lifestyle, claiming that it leads to closeness to God through enlightenment. Sufism gave the world many outstanding philosophers and scholars, such as Al-Junaid Baghdadi who died in the year 911, and Al-Ghazali, who died in the year 1111. Al-Ghazali was one of the most original philosophers of his time as well as a famous theologian. Very famous was also Ibn Sina, or Avisenna, who died in the year 1037. Ibn Sina was the author of the book *Al-Shifa*, or the *Book of Treatments*, which was the encyclopedia of knowledge of the eleventh century, starting with medicine and ending with philosophy as well as mathematics, which enlightened medieval Europe at the time. Sufis were predominantly organised into four Orders: Order of Chishty, Order of Kadiry, Order of Suhravardy and Order of Nakshbandy. Abu Iskhak Chishty, sometimes called 'The Syrian', was born in the tenth century and was a Seyd, or the descendant of Prophet Muhammed PBUH. This Order was organised in the settlement of Chishty in Khorasan and used music widely for its exercises. The wandering dervishes of this Order of Chishty would arrive at a settlement and put up an exotic display accompanied by moving sounds of flutes and drumbeats, gathering the inhabitants for the spectacle. Members of the Order of Chishty eventually turned into wandering musicians, especially popular during those times in India. The Order of Kadiry was organised by the followers of Abu-Kadir Gilani, who was born in the settlement of Nif in Gilan located to the South of the Caspian Sea. He died in 1166, leaving behind terminology and methods of entering into a transcendental meditation state for his students. The Order of Suhravardy was founded by Ziauddin Suhravardy in the twelfth century and became well known in India, Iran and Africa. Sheikh Ziauddin left behind an expression: 'Self-justification is worth more than the original fault. The main and most well known Order of the Sufis was the Order of Nakshbandy. It is believed that this Order was the earliest and most influential. It gave the medieval world many outstanding philosophers as well as rulers. It was founded by Hoja Bahauddin Nakshbandy, who passed away in the year 1389. The followers of Bahauddin never distinguished themselves from ordinary people and were respected for their honesty and piousness. As a result, a tradition was formed over the centuries that became customary to add the word 'Sufy' in front of the name of such people to emphasise their pious status. When answering a question, 'What is Sufism?' the Sufis sometimes refer to the following statement by Prophet Muhammed: 'Talk to a person in line with that person's capacity to understand what you are saying.' This is their way of communicating as the person asking about Sufism may not get the right impression about Sufism if that person's intellect is not at the same level as the respondent's. Sufism, therefore, attempts to teach by offering practical examples. One of them is quoted:

One person appeared to have died, so all around him made arrangements to bury him. Suddenly, he became alive, but seeing that they made arrangements to bury him, he fainted again out of fright. He was then put into a coffin and carried to the cemetery. When the coffin bearers reached the cemetery, he woke up again and lifting the top of the coffin started to call for help. 'He cannot be alive,' said the mourners. 'A competent doctor has issued a Certificate of Death for him.' 'But I am alive!' shouted the person in the coffin. He appealed to a well-known lawyer who turned up for the burial. 'Just a second,' said the lawyer. He counted all those who were present at the burial site and asked, 'You all heard what this person is saying, whom you all came to bury. You fifty witnesses tell me, what do you think is true?' 'But he died,' uttered the witnesses. 'Bury him!' ordered the lawyer. So, the man was buried. Although this story is shocking, in everyday life there are many examples of such irrational behaviour of a crowd.

Prophet Muhammed once declared: 'Stupid people cause more harm because of their stupidity than evil-doers can cause because of their evilness.' The Hadis, or compilation of the utterances of Prophet Muhammed, has many examples of his special respect towards scholars, and of his struggle with ignorance and stubbornness. Prophet Muhammed often appealed to Muslims to strive for continuous learning, especially in the field of natural sciences. Once, he declared:

'Strive for learning, even if you have to travel to China to achieve that!' China then was regarded by the Arabs as a very distant and mysterious country far away in the East. It is therefore especially important for Muslims to always keep learning to improve their knowledge by educating themselves in everyday life. It is appropriate to end this brief and rather superficial presentation about the teachings of Islam by quoting from a chapter of the philosophical works of Ahmed Yasawi titled, *About Your Religion*:

> As you familiarise yourself with the literature of the Sufis, you shall learn once more that we are not interested in your religion or even its absence. How could this be equated with the fact that the believers always think that they are the God's chosen people? The main aim is to enlighten all the people and all religious teachings should strive to achieve this aim. To achieve this aim there is a tradition of passing the knowledge from one generation to another, and chosen ones then become the carriers of this knowledge. The knowledge is spread among many people and nations. As we are adherents of the essential philosophy, we direct all those who chose the right path to keep expanding their knowledge in its pure form. Dogmatic expressions of Judaism, Christianity, Zoroastrianism, Hinduism, and even Islam, have lost this precious aim. We return this vital principle to all these religions. That is why you will discover so many Jews, Christians and others among my disciples.

These Jews tell us that we are the real Jews, and Christians that we are the Christians. Only when you discover the essence of God's existence, you shall learn about the real purpose of the modern religions and even atheism. After all, even atheism is a religion with its own system of beliefs.

2

East Turkestan Reflections

My grandfather on my father's side, Salih Sadriddinov, was an entrepreneur who escaped into East Turkestan with his wife to avoid being recruited into the Imperial Russian army as a slave soldier subject to 25-year compulsory service prior to 1905. Once settled down in the Kuldja District of the Yily Valley, he became the first entrepreneur to introduce bee-keeping into the mountains of the region harvesting high-quality honey from the wildflowers abundant in the summertime in the mountains there. He was also the first to experiment with breeding mountain deer to harvest their horns for the production of deer antler extract, highly prized by Chinese traditional medicine as an aphrodisiac.

He was also among the first to build a downstream water-driven, flour-grinding mill to produce high-quality wheat flour for the local population. All these ventures enabled him to import from Germany and build a high-tech, animal hide processing plant, producing high-quality leather and leather goods such as leather shoes and leather saddles.

He was successful in these entrepreneurial pursuits to the

point where the book titled, *Strany Vostoka* (Countries of the East), published in 1932 in Russia, listed in its section on Sinkiang my grandfather's surname as one of the five wealthy families with de facto control of the economic activities in East Turkestan. He, nonetheless, ended up losing a substantial part of his wealth by fulfilling a Chinese army order for 2,000 full sets of leather saddles and other implements to equip a full Chinese Cavalry regiment, only to end up not getting paid a single cent by the Chinese army, as it was then disintegrating and fleeing out of Xinjiang. As a result of this economic fiasco, as well as the political turmoil that followed, he was forced to shut down the leather processing plant.

It subsequently turned out to be a blessing in disguise for him, as he ended up not being classified as a 'capitalist' by the incoming Chinese communist regime, thereby avoiding the fate of many other 'capitalists' who were taken out and publicly executed by the Chinese communist troops in a frenzied display of orchestrated mass hysteria to frighten the rest of the local population into total subservience.

Once the Chinese communist regime established itself in the province, my grandfather decided to accept a Soviet Russian citizenship passport as a form of protection against the excesses of the local Chinese communist regime. Time showed later, years down the track, that this decision was to have far-reaching negative repercussions on our entire extended family's bid to migrate to the free world rather than repatriating to the Soviet Union.

On my mother's side our ancestral lineage ascends to Tatar Mirza nobility, who were Sayeds, or descendants of Prophet Muhammed PBUH—a Tatar nobility with overseas roots, as my mother's fabulously rich merchant grandfather, Sharafuddin Haji Gabitov, married Miss Bibi Gafifa Banu—my grandfather, Sayed Muhammed Garif Gabitov's, mother—who was a descendant of the Prophet Muhammed. They lived in a large, two-storey mansion in the centre of the city of Kazan, where the first ever Tatar theatre was played in the early 1900s. My grandfather on my mother's side, Mirza Sayed Muhammed Garif, was a colourful figure who studied at the Kazan University but was prevented from getting his graduation diploma as the price of getting a graduation diploma prior to the revolution of 1905 was formal conversion into Russian Orthodox Christianity, which he was not willing to accept on moral grounds. As a university graduate without a diploma, he was, nonetheless, employed to teach at an exclusive college in Kuldja, East Turkestan, where he ended up as a result of political upheavals in Russia in 1905, where his famous, wealthy, merchant father Sharafuddin Haji Gabitov had extensive properties and business trading interests as well as houses and upmarket stone-built shops. Even if he had to escape to Kuldja as a result of the failed revolution of 1905, he had an enjoyable lifestyle there working as a school principal, hunting and fishing in his free time and occasionally pushing progressive revolutionary speeches at public gatherings and rallies in Kuldja.

It should be noted here that prior to 1905 oppressive

policies of the Russian Empire, orchestrated by Konstantin Pobedonostsev of the Russian Orthodox Church's Holy Synod, especially targeted the Tatar, Jewish and other non-Russian educated class citizens into forced 25-year slave-like army service, driving, as a result, most of them into revolutionary action to depose the Russian Imperial regime.

By denying Tatar and Jewish university graduates a diploma and therefore a chance to gain a well-paid occupation, unless they converted into the Russian Orthodox Church, the Imperial Russian State and the Russian Orthodox Church's Holy Synod turned them into their mortal enemies.

This fact explains why there were such a large number of highly educated Tatar as well as Jewish revolutionaries determined to demolish the Imperial Russian regime, such as Mirsaid Sultan-Galiev, Sayed Ismail Gabitov, or Leon Trotsky (Bronstein), all of them struggling to depose the Imperial regime in Russia and to establish a communist regime with a 'human face', but in the end, all of them were annihilated by the ruthless mass murderer Joseph Stalin.

Mrs Bibi Gafifa Banu—my grandfather, Sayed Muhammed Garif Gabitov's, mother—was of Prophet Muhammed's lineage PBUH, thus bestowing her sons Ismail and Garif with the honorary titles of Sayed, or descendants of the Prophet Muhammed PBUH. In Islamic culture, the honorary titles of Sayed for men or Sayeda for women, were customarily bestowed to both male and female descendants of the Prophet Muhammed PBUH as he had only daughters and no sons to continue his lineage.

My great-grandfather, Sharafuddin Haji Gabitov, enlisted the support of the local wealthy people and built the Kashefiyeh College consisting of four classrooms and ten boarding rooms for students in the city of Kuldja in 1895, thus making a very important contribution to the education of the local Tatar as well as Uighur, Uzbek and Kazakh youths, who then played an important role in uplifting educational and cultural standards of the local population.

My maternal grandfather, Sayed Muhammed Garif Gabitov, was born in 1884 in Kazan and succeeded in studying at Kazan University until the revolution of 1905. During the repressions that followed the failed uprising of 1905, he had to escape to Kuldja and ended up working there as a teacher and school principal of the college opened by his father, Sharafuddin Haji Gabitov, in 1895.

By 1913 he was then a 28-year-old college teacher and freelance revolutionary orator. He succeeded in attracting one of his students—my grandmother, Aysha—a beautiful and highly intelligent 17-year-old blonde, and persuaded her to abscond from her house and marry him against her mother's wishes because her mother wanted her to marry an elderly religious figure, or Mullah.

My grandmother Aysha's mother, Maymuna Abestay, herself highly educated in religious matters, bluntly told my grandfather, Garif Gabitov—when he came to ask for her daughter's hand in marriage—that she would not accept a long-haired, Russian-educated school teacher as her son-in-law. So, my grandmother, Aysha, decided to marry my grandfather, Sayed Muhammed Garif Gabitov, in secret against her domineering mother's wishes in 1913.

After their first son—my uncle, Sayed Azrael Gabitov—was born in 1914, they decided to go back to Kazan in Russia in early 1917 to attend to my great-grandmother's health, or eyesight problems. That was a fateful decision because shortly after their arrival in Kazan, the 1917 revolution broke out.

One evening in late August 1918, my maternal grandfather, Sayed Muhammed Garif Gabitov, was called out from the family mansion by his revolutionary colleagues and disappeared into the blue mist, leaving behind his heavily pregnant, beautiful young wife as well as his infant son. He was never heard of ever again, despite my grandmother Aysha's subsequent desperate attempts over many years to locate him and find out what had happened to him. In the turmoil of the revolution, followed by the civil war, there was complete chaos in Kazan with wanton killings on both sides, resulting in Kazan's changing of hands several times between Bolshevik 'Reds' and their 'White' adversaries.

The civil war ended up getting badly aggravated by food shortages and mass hunger among the population, with lots of dead bodies often lying in the streets of Kazan with nobody bothering to collect and bury them.

When my grandmother, Aysha, first cradled my newborn mother, Lailya, in her hands in October 1918, she cried in despair, 'My unfortunate, poor baby, why have you come into this cruel world? Your father is now gone for more than a month, no news of him of any kind, the house is cold, no food to eat, death everywhere and human life is now worthless.'

My great-grandmother, Hafifa Banu, then consoled her. 'Do not cry, my child, this baby will be very fortunate. There is celebration in our house. Ibrahim just delivered firewood, your workplace sent you bread, flour, oil and even one box of chocolates. The baby is lucky. Cheer up and be happy,' she told my grandmother, Aysha. As a talented writer and publisher, my grandmother was then working in one of the major publishing houses in Kazan. She went back to work and my mother was cared for by my grandfather's elder sister, Zainab Teregulova.

As living conditions in Kazan kept worsening, my grandmother's uncle, Shamsuddin Husseinov, who was living in one of the distant villages not yet affected by food shortages and the resultant hunger, took my grandmother and her two young children to his village to live in his house. My grandmother, Aysha, with her little baby—my mother, Lailya—and my uncle—her infant son, Azrael—lived in his household for several months during the worst period of hunger in Kazan.

Once the situation in Kazan slightly improved, she decided to return to her family home in Kazan. Once back in Kazan, she discovered that the authorities were looking for a headmistress to take some 80 orphaned girls—whose parents had died of participation in the civil war, or of hunger—to Chardzhou in Turkmenistan, where there was no shortage of food, whereas acute famine continued in the Volga region. My grandmother, Aysha, took up the challenge and volunteered to take the orphans there. During the train trip there, most of the orphans contracted typhus and fell ill. By the time they reached Chardzhou, the entire group had contracted typhus, including my grandmother. Somehow, they managed to survive the typhus and settled in Chardzhou to continue with their high school education, developing a great attachment to my grandmother as their headmistress. In summer they would often go to the banks of the river Amu Darya for a swim. My three-year-old mother, Lailya, seeing how the girls—who were all skilful swimmers having grown up on the banks of the Volga River—were jumping into the river from the high embankment, asked my grandmother, 'Mummy, may I jump as well?' to which my grandmother replied, 'Of course, little monkey,' without expecting that she would indeed jump into the fast-flowing river. My then three-year-old mother jumped into the river to be carried away by the fast-flowing current. All the girls present jumped into the river after her and managed to somehow locate her in the water and rescued her, to the great relief of my grandmother.

After working there for well over two years, my grandmother decided to take up long-term leave and travel to Tashkent in Uzbekistan, where her lost husband's elder brother, Sayed Ismail Gabitov, was then living. Prior to the revolution, Ismail Gabitov had worked as editor and publisher of *Taraki* until the publication was ceased by the Tsarist regime of the time. Given all the turmoil of the ongoing civil war and the resultant insecurity in the region, he advised my grandmother to take her two children—my mother, Lailya, and Uncle Azrael—and go back to Kuldja in East Turkestan where there were still substantial extended family real estate assets available to support her and her two little children.

My grandmother, Aysha, decided to take up his advice and support, travelling further east where she managed to cross the sparsely guarded border near Yarkend (Panfilov) safely with her eight-year-old son, Azrael, and four-year-old daughter, Lailya, arriving in Kuldja in 1923.

Once settled in Kuldja, she managed to claim and to inherit some of her extended family's real estate and shop assets in order to live above the subsistence level and without much economic hardship.

She always waited for and longed to see her beloved husband, Sayed Muhammed Garif Gabitov, who disappeared without a trace after leaving the family home in Kazan at the end of August 1918.

My grandmother, Aysha, died early on 31 March 1936 at the age of thirty-eight of complications from a stomach ulcer aggravated by bronchitis in early March due to a lack of proper medical treatment available in Kuldja at the time. When my mother and uncle requested a transit visa via the Soviet Union to take my grandmother, Aysha, to Turkey or western Europe for treatment from the Soviet consulate in Kuldja in 1935, the Soviet consular officials bluntly refused to provide them with the transit visas needed to travel to Turkey or Western Europe, although many other wealthy local Uighurs were routinely getting transit visas to travel to Turkey. The most likely reason was that in 1935–36, Red Army General Sayed Ismail Gabitov was already in disgrace—being associated with Leon Trotsky and getting demoted by Stalin to be shot later alongside many other senior Red Army generals—so his relatives living in Kuldja were also treated by the Soviet diplomats there as *personae non grata.*

Many years later I learned from the memoirs of Burhan Shaheedy, who played an important role in the political landscape of Xinjiang as a minister in several successive governments of the region, that Sayed Muhammed Garif Gabitov was assigned the task of starting an uprising against the White Army forces in West Turkestan—which included Uzbekistan, Turkmenistan, Kazakhstan as well as the Kuldja region in East Turkestan—and was ordered to go there together with six of his comrades at the end of August 1918 from Kazan. Somehow, he was compelled to obey the order as a member of the revolutionary Red Cell, leaving behind his heavily pregnant young wife and infant son. This premature, brainless task assigned to the recruited Tatar 'Red Revolutionaries' was obviously doomed to fail from the start because General Dutov's Russian 'White' Army detachments in Turkestan were then still actively controlling the region. Somehow, they succeeded in stopping and capturing together all seven Tatar 'Red Revolutionaries', including my grandfather, Sayed Muhammed Garif Gabitov, strip-searched them and discovered their identity documents and a mandate to start a military uprising in the Turkestan region against the 'White' Russian forces.

So, in a brazen display of wanton cruelty prevalent in those lawless times, they murdered all seven of their Tatar captives by burying them alive in one grave, thus ending their brainless venture before it even started.

The seven Tatar revolutionaries' tragic deaths were of little value and did not serve any useful purpose, but the full Red Army control of Central Asia was, nonetheless, achieved in the early 1920s under the supreme command of Leon Trotsky who was then a brilliant military strategist responsible for the defeat of the 'White' military forces during the then ongoing civil war.

'White' General Dutov eventually ended up paying with his own life for this atrocity of his subordinates. One of the comrades of the seven revolutionary commanders buried alive—Kasym Khan—dressed himself in a senior 'White' Army officer's uniform and turned up one morning on the army horseback at General Dutov's headquarters in Kuldja, dismounted his horse, threw the reins to the general's guards who had hastily approached him and ordered them to tie the horse up as he had to deliver an urgent secret package to General Dutov himself. As his horse was being led away and tied up by General Dutov's guards, he calmly walked into the general's room, shot him in the head—as well as the general's aide-de-camp present in the room—with his Mauser pistol, turned around and shot three other guards outside before they managed to draw their weapons, jumped on his horse and galloped away. In total confusion and disarray, the 'White' Army soldiers did not even manage to mount a proper chase after him in broad daylight.

The irony of it all is the fact that this brave Red Army Tatar officer's heroic action did not even get proper recognition anywhere and the officer himself ended up eventually perishing in Stalin's death camps in 1938.

Nonetheless, this outstanding accomplishment that pacified the entire Turkestan region and delivered it into Soviet hands, did not save him from eventually getting executed by Stalin during Stalin's purges of the Red Army senior commanders in 1937–38, being accused of affiliation with Leon Trotsky, who, unlike Stalin, then just simply an obscure Bolshevik Party backroom apparatchik, played a key role during the civil war in Russia in defeating the 'Whites' as a brilliant military strategist, but ended up running for his life out of communist Russia after getting defeated by scheming Stalin during internal Communist (Bolshevik) Party struggles.

Stalin, after first getting his closest comrade, Sergei Kirov, assassinated, then accused his other potential rivals in the communist hierarchy—Lev Kamenev, Grigory Zinovyev, Nikolay Bukharin and Aleksey Rykov—of plotting his assassination, extracted from them false confessions by torturing them and finished them all off, thus setting the stage for the great purges of 1935–38, when more than two million Communist Party officials, military commanders as well as educated upper and middle-class citizens lost their lives on Stalin's orders. Then Stalin decided to finish off Leon Trotsky as well by dispatching an assassin to Mexico in August 1940, who chopped up Leon Trotsky with an axe whilst Trotsky was living a lonely and miserable life in exile in Mexico.

3

East Turkestan turned into Xinjiang of China on Stalin's Orders

From 1945 until 1950 the entire population of the newly self-declared Republic of East Turkestan incorporating three regions—Yily, Altay, and Tarbagatay—enjoyed economic prosperity as well as political freedoms not experienced for a long time. After the Armistice of 1945 and the agreement reached in Urumchi (Urumqi) on 2 January 1946 to form a coalition government with the remnants of the KMT leadership there, the detachments of the East Turkestan army entered the capital city of Xinjiang, Urumchi, impressing observers with their military training and high spirits. My father, Sagit Sadriddinov, then the officer of the East Turkestan Army in the rank of Major, which had defeated the Chinese Nationalist Army detachments in East Turkestan, was getting demobilised and embarking on a commercial trading carrier. My mother, Lailya Sadriddinova, was then practising as a successful dentist with her own dental practice. Virtually the entire adult population participated in the war effort against the Nationalist Chinese Army detachments in East Turkestan in 1944–1945 as a response to the atrocities that had been committed by them at the time against the local population, especially against immigrants from Russia. My father, Sagit Sadriddinov, who spoke fluent Russian after getting educated earlier as a foreign student at Central Asian State University in Tashkent under the assumed surname Jusaev in order to conceal his wealthy parents' identity, after he had to return home once the Second World War (WW2) started in Europe in 1939, was entrusted with the important task of negotiating with the Soviet leadership and physically delivering to the Eastern Turkestan Army detachments fighting at the frontline truckloads of mostly German-made, second-hand arms and ammunition captured by the Soviet Army on the front, as it was advancing against Hitler's occupational forces. In return, East Turkestan rebels were paying back the Soviet side for the armaments supplied by delivering large quantities of livestock, foodstuffs and wheat—badly needed by the Soviet regime. When not working on arms deliveries to the front, Sagit Sadriddinov was in charge of counter-intelligence operations at the army headquarters. His younger sister, Dr Shafika Sadriddinova, served at the frontline as a doctor and was highly decorated with military medals for saving many wounded soldiers' lives, whereas my mother, Lailya Sadriddinova, did the same by undertaking reconstructive surgery of wounded soldiers' jaws and faces, brought back from the frontline, suffering from shrapnel and bullet wounds.

Born post-war on 1 July 1946, I remember my early years growing up in a fairly affluent extended family household and being looked after by a Russian-speaking domestic nanny as an infant, whilst my mother was busy working as a dentist in her dental surgery.

The Republic of East Turkestan run by the native leadership under the subtle guidance of Soviet 'advisers', offered a few years of both political and economic freedoms as well as respite from the Chinese colonial oppression of the local population perpetrated on them prior to the local population's uprising in November 1944. From 1945–1950, after defeating and expelling the Chinese KMT armed forces from East Turkestan, the local native population enjoyed economic as well as political freedoms under the banner of the Republic of East Turkestan.

The East Turkestan leadership, however, did not have the foresight or the ability to exert full independence from the Soviet 'advisers'. Their days of freedom and a good life free from Chinese oppression turned out to be short-lived as a result of a political deal reached between Mao and Stalin in Moscow in 1950, with Mao pledging and convincing Stalin that China under his leadership would commit to remain firmly under Stalin's control and guidance into the future, as long as the free Republic of East Turkestan was liquidated and returned to full communist Chinese control, as it would otherwise offer a permanent example and a temptation for the leadership of the Soviet Republics of West Turkestan to strive to seek freedom as well and to exit eventually from the Soviet Union.

Stalin somehow succumbed to Mao's arguments about reverting East Turkestan to communist Chinese control, and decided to liquidate the fledgling Republic of East Turkestan.

The Republic of East Turkestan was therefore liquidated on Stalin's orders at the end of 1949–early 1950, with its leadership—namely chief leader Ali Khan Ture—being kidnapped by the Soviet NKVD agents to be taken across the border into Uzbekistan to be detained there, whereas other key leaders of the East Turkestan government headed by Ahmetjan Kasimi and General Iskhakbek were flown to Beijing under the pretext of negotiating the terms of their independence or autonomy with Chairman Mao's communist regime.

A few days after their departure, an announcement was made that their aircraft crashed en route to Beijing somewhere over the Soviet territory. In reality, they were all detained by the Mao regime upon arrival in Beijing with Stalin's consent.

They were all kept in secret detention, eventually dying in Mao's prisons in Beijing in the1960s alongside more than 50 million Chinese victims who were starved to death by Mao in his so-called 're-education labour' concentration camps as well as a result of his experimentation with 'Great Leap Forward', 'Communisation of Agriculture' and 'Eradication of Middle-Class Enemies' campaigns. The last surviving members of the East Turkestan government were murdered in prison in Beijing in 1966 during the start-up of Mao's so-called 'Cultural revolution'.

My earliest memories involve remembering the arrival of the Chinese Red Army detachments in 1950, when the locals and especially the local Uighur women were initially impressed by their friendliness and willingness to help even with their domestic chores such as chopping firewood for them or fetching bucketloads of drinking water from the deep-water wells.

Once the Chinese Red Army detachments and the Chinese communist administration firmly settled in and assumed full control, such friendliness was abruptly transformed into wanton brutality in 1951–1952, with mass imprisonments of the former members of the East Turkestan Army as well as the affluent and well-educated members of the local middle-class and so-called 'capitalists', who were accused by the Chinese communist regime of being 'class enemies and exploiters of the people'.

In this context it is worth noting that the Chiang Kai-shek (Chiang Jieshi) regime's former military commander in East Turkestan, General Tao Se Ya, who was defeated by the Soviet-sponsored and equipped East Turkestan Army in 1944–1945, turned up in 1950 in Xinjiang (East Turkestan) as the Chinese Red Army general in charge of the occupying communist regime forces. This is because after getting defeated and expelled from East Turkestan, he decided to switch sides by abandoning the Kuomintang (KMT) with his surviving troops and joining Mao Zedong's victorious Red Army. Chairman Mao obviously decided to use General Tao's knowledge of local conditions in East Turkestan for the benefit of the Chinese Red Army re-occupation effort.

Naturally, General Tao Se Ya was also keen to take revenge on his now disarmed and helpless former enemies, by first imprisoning them *en masse*, then as a form of scornful and humiliating punishment forcing them to be substituted for beasts of burden in pulling horse carts, ploughing land and eventually executing them one by one as 'war criminals' during staged mass show trials alongside other so-called 'class enemies and capitalists', whose wealth and properties were then confiscated by the Chinese communist regime for their own benefit.

These show trials were accompanied by staged mass rallies, where many thousands of local inhabitants were chased out of their homes in order to participate in the rallies. They were ordered to shout obscenities at the bound and gagged victims, who were then executed in front of the hysterically roaring crowds loudly pretending to demand their execution.

In between these hysterical episodes of staged mass show trials, the Chinese authorities were methodically imprisoning not only senior officers of the former East Turkestan Army, but also anybody deemed to be rich, well-educated, and non-receptive to the Chinese Communist Party rule. This wanton and unbridled oppression of the upper classes of the local population continued unabated from 1950 until the height of the Korean War in 1952, when the Chinese communist rulers felt insecure enough and resorted even to appealing to the local population to surrender their gold jewellery and valuables to contribute to the war effort against the South Koreans and the United Nations forces fighting them in Korea. By then, the Chinese Red Army in Korea was rumoured to have lost more than 1 million soldiers, including even Chairman Mao's own son.

Frightened local women competed with one another to take their jewellery and valuables to the collection points in order to appease the Chinese communist regime. It was towards the end of the Korean War in 1953 and after Stalin's death that the Chinese communist authorities decided to somewhat relax their policies nationwide and let the population in East Turkestan as well enjoy a sign of relative relief. This meant that the local population was once again allowed to go about their everyday business activities cultivating crops, raising livestock, manufacturing goods for their everyday necessities as well as trading in the markets without fearing that their merchandise could be confiscated. This temporary policy of relative economic freedom lasted for close to five years from Stalin's death in March 1953 until September 1958.

4

Post-Stalin Era in East Turkestan under Chinese Rule

I vividly remember as a six-year-old boy the day Stalin's death was announced in Kuldja in early March 1953. I was told then that a siren would sound for three minutes to commemorate his burial time and that everybody was supposed to freeze, standing in silence when the siren sounded. Once I heard the siren, I was curious to see the people frozen to a standstill in the street and so ran out to see them.

To my disappointment, the usually busy street outside our house was absolutely empty, as frightened people hid themselves in their houses rather than risk being seen outside in the streets and getting accused of failing to properly observe three minutes of silence. When I got back into the house, my mother reprimanded me for going outside, saying that they could get into trouble for my failing to hide inside our house and standing still for the duration of the loudly howling siren.

From 1953 until 1957, I remember myself leading a peaceful life in a relatively affluent family and going to a Russian language school ironically named a 'Stalin High School', where I academically excelled as one of the best students both in terms of school work as well as being the school's champion chess player by defeating even the provincial chess champion during the Xinjiang State Chess Championships, at which I represented our school.

The two-month-long summer vacation time was especially enjoyable as we went to our summer house in the picturesque Talky Mountains en route to Lake Sayram surrounded by the mountains on all sides. The Talky Mountains were sparsely populated in the summer months then (and still in pristine condition), where we lived next to the family apiary, catching mountain trout abundant in the cool rivulets running down the mountain gorges, collecting delicious wild strawberries and raspberries abundant on the Talky mountain slopes next to natural granite quarries, collecting delicious wild apricots as well to make jam or dry them out for winter, or even cutting up and drying out small wild apples which were not as delicious as wild apricots or wild strawberries or raspberries, but, nonetheless, were very tasty when cut and dried out to be preserved and consumed in the winter months.

In early autumn prior to returning to the city of Kuldja to

the start of the school season on September 1st, we would occasionally go out and hunt for mountain partridges, or get up very early in the morning to go higher up the mountains and hunt for black mountain grouses that would occasionally congregate on select remote mountain clearances at dawn to start their playful cock-fights, presumably to shed excess energy as well as to attract the attention of female grouses that sat on surrounding trees to observe the fighting cocks. Sometimes my older brothers did succeed in shooting one or two of them to be brought home, plucked, cleaned by our mother and cooked as a delicious wild game meal, stewed by mixing the game bird's meat with carrots, potatoes, wild mountain onions and garlic. The pristine Talky Mountains then were only frequented in summer by Kazakh nomads with their sheep or cattle and horses, but remained relatively untouched and unspoiled by human hands. There was an abundance of wild mountain animals as well, such as wild mountain goats, mountain deer, and even the occasional brown bear. Higher slopes above 3,000 metres even accommodated occasional wild sheep (mouflons) as well as large mountain deer prized for their antlers by Chinese medicine as an aphrodisiac.

Being an ex-military man, our father bought for my two older brothers and me either a rifle or a shotgun. I remember getting a small Belgian-made .22 rifle when still only nine years old and quickly learning to become quite a skilful shooter with it, although I was allowed primarily to go out on my own and catch mountain trout, or to collect wild apricots, strawberries and raspberries.

In 1957 my parents decided to sell our apiary in the Talky Mountains as well as their house in the city of Kuldja and relocate to Central China hoping to emigrate to Australia from there. During his previous trip to Shanghai in 1955, my father found out that many Russian emigres as well as other Europeans resident in Harbin and Shanghai were getting visas to migrate to Australia, Canada, South America or Turkey, instead of going back to the Soviet Union as many others were doing at the time after succumbing to the pressure to repatriate from the pro-Soviet local authorities. By then in Xinjiang, mass repatriation of former emigres from Russia was in full swing, being encouraged by the local authorities to re-settle into the vast open landmass of Kazakhstan by getting dumped there to build their own dwellings and to start their collective kolkhoz farm crop production—in most cases with miserable results—until eventually getting permission to re-locate and succeeding in moving into one of the bigger cities like Alma Ata, Tashkent, Bishkek or Kazan.

The Chinese communist regime's atrocities and mass public executions committed in 1951–52 towards the population of East Turkestan were still fresh in people's minds, when the Chinese communist regime singled out the well-educated and well-off segment of the local population, especially the emigres who had originally settled into East Turkestan after escaping from the Bolshevik atrocities committed in West Turkestan and Russia proper under Stalin's rule. For them going back to the Soviet Union appeared to be the lesser of two evils, rather than ending up starving in Chinese agricultural communes or forced labour concentration camps.

My parents—my father by then a successful businessman, and my mother a successful dentist with her own dental practice—decided not to get repatriated to the Soviet Union to end up getting dumped onto the vast expanses of Kazakhstan's steppes (tselina/virgin land) to start from scratch as agricultural workers in a Soviet kolkhoz (Agricultural Collective Production Farm), but to try to re-locate to Central China and apply for a migration visa to Australia. They had sufficient funds derived from the sale of their apiary in the Talky Mountains as well as their house in the city of Kuldja, in addition to their liquid assets to cover not only relocation costs but also to be reasonably well-off upon arrival in Australia. Our family boarded a small passenger plane to fly across vast expanses of Xinjiang into Lanzhou, the provincial capital of Gansu Province, where there was a railway line to take our family to Peking, the capital city of Communist China.

Upon arrival in Peking, we had an enjoyable one-month stay in a good, clean hotel, visiting museums, art galleries, and tourist shops, eating our meals in good restaurants and enjoying ourselves visiting numerous public attractions and parks.

The capital city of Beijing in Communist China

in 1957—prior to Chairman Mao's embarking in the autumn of 1958 on oppressive measures such as large-scale misappropriation of private assets, communisation of the agricultural sector and mass incarceration of so-called 'upper classes' of citizens—was quite an enjoyable place to visit and spend leisurely time overall, leaving very fond memories for myself, then an impressionable eleven-year-old boy.

After one month my parents decided to move to Shanghai in order to try to get an entry visa for Australia and apply for an exit visa to migrate there. Upon arrival in Shanghai by train from Peking, we were met at the railway station by my father's younger brother, who had moved to Shanghai a couple of years earlier. He accompanied us and checked us into Jing Gang Fan Dian, then one of the few five-star hotels in Shanghai. Shortly after our arrival my parents went to the offices of the British Chargé d'Affaires in Shanghai, where the officials there told my mother—who could speak reasonable English—that an entry visa application to Australia may take more than a year to process and that there were quite a few Russian families from Sinkiang (Xinjiang), living in the outer suburb of Shanghai called Hung Jiao Lu, struggling to survive while waiting for their entry visas to Australia. They suggested that given our reasonably affluent background, perhaps an entry visa for Turkey could be much quicker for us to obtain from the Turkish Embassy in Tokyo, Japan, rather than waiting for a protracted period of time for the Australian entry visa, which was not that easy to obtain even then, despite the existence of the ongoing 'White Russian Refugee Resettlement Program into Australia' from China.

So, my parents filed an application for a visa to migrate to Turkey. To everybody's astonishment, the entry visa for our family to go to Turkey arrived at the British Chargé d'Affaires' office in Shanghai after just 23 days, paving the way for our family to apply for the exit visa to go from Shanghai to Hong Kong from the communist Chinese authorities. Apparently, the Turkish Embassy in Tokyo was surprised by our family's application to migrate to Turkey from East Turkestan and issued entry visas forthwith.

The Officer-in-Charge at the British Chargé d'Affaires office must also have been impressed by the fact that my mother could communicate in English, so he had offered to help with the exit visa application to the Chinese Foreign Affairs office in Shanghai, saying that they had established good contacts with the Chinese officials in charge there and could get us exit visas relatively quickly, within a few weeks. My mother wanted to ask them to proceed with our exit visa application, but my father flatly refused to apply for the exit visa, saying that he wanted to wait for the arrival of his parents and two sisters with their families in Shanghai from Xinjiang (East Turkestan) and only then migrate to Turkey together with his extended family members.

This turned out to be a fateful mistake because a golden

opportunity to leave China when it was still a relatively free political environment in the summer of 1957, was lost irrevocably.

One of the Chinese Foreign Affairs officials in Shanghai even went to the trouble of visiting our family while we were still living in the five-star Jing Jiang Fan Dian Hotel, politely asking my mother in English if we needed any help with securing our exit visas. Once again, my father insisted that we should wait for his parents to arrive in Shanghai before applying for the exit visas together with them. It took several months for our extended family—my grandparents and aunties—to arrive in Shanghai. By the time they eventually arrived and obtained their entry visas into Turkey, several precious months of a politically-free environment were irrevocably lost. My father's extended family members also happened to turn up in Shanghai with their Soviet passports in their pockets, which complicated the issue of exit visas by the Chinese authorities because it turned out that, according to the Chinese authorities, Soviet citizens were supposed to obtain the consent of the Soviet General Consulate in Shanghai for the Chinese authorities to issue exit visas to the Soviet citizens to leave to 'capitalist' countries such as Turkey or Australia rather than repatriating back to the Soviet Union. The Soviet General Consulate in Shanghai refused to issue such consent, suggesting that the extended Sadriddinov family members were highly respected Soviet citizens in East Turkestan and therefore should repatriate back to the Soviet Union as an example for others to follow.

Although my parents did not have Soviet passports and were holding Stateless Refugee Certificates at the time, they were regarded as part of the extended family with Soviet citizenship, so the British Chargé d'Affaires office was no longer able to help us with obtaining exit visas. By then they had also lost their friendly contacts in the Chinese Foreign Office in Shanghai, which was subjected to extensive purges as part of the political tightening in Communist China in 1958.

Towards the autumn of 1957 my parents managed to rent a small, one-bedroom apartment and moved out of Jing Jiang Fan Dian. I was enrolled to study English in a private British school together with my younger sister, Nailya. Early every morning the two of us would run to the bus stop, board a bus and travel for half an hour to get to the British school run by British missionaries, Mr King, Mr John, Mr Evans and Mr Koo. We managed to attend that school for over one year until the autumn of 1958, learning good English as well as maths and geography. One day in the autumn of 1958, Mr King called me into his office and told me that he was sorry to warn me that the Chinese authorities were planning to arrest my father as well as his younger brother and brother-in-law in order to exile us all back into Xinjiang.

I went home and told my parents Mr King's message, but probably it did not sink well into my father's mind, or more likely he simply did not know what to do. A few days later, several Chinese policemen turned up and arrested my father. All our suitcases were also sealed by them and we were all told to get ready to depart back to Xinjiang. Not long after that, several policemen arrived to take us all—five Tatar families—back to Xinjiang.

In 1958, Chairman Mao and his comrades came up with a brilliant idea, declaring, 'Let the hundred flowers blossom and let the hundred birds sing,' encouraging the entire population, especially the educated and the well-off members of Chinese society nationwide, to speak up their minds by criticising the Communist Party rule and making suggestions on how to improve the governance of the Communist Party in order to create more freedoms as well as economic prosperity for the country.

Many educated citizens took Chairman Mao's appeal at its face value and flooded the meetings and the official press with criticisms of Chairman Mao's Communist Party regime. All their uttering as well as their written presentations were carefully recorded and kept by Chairman Mao's secret service agents. Then suddenly, after a few months of such 'singing', in the autumn of 1958 and on Chairman Mao's orders, all the 'singers' who did not keep their mouths shut were rounded up *en masse* into 're-education by labour' concentration camps, where gradual death of the inmates through starvation and long hours of exhausting hard labour was a carefully planned and executed outcome.

Even official Chinese statistical records depict a drastic reduction in population numbers, which shows that more than 50 million people in China overall lost their lives in the period of 1958–1963 as a result of the 'Great Leap Forward', 'Re-education by Labour' and 'Overtaking England in Steel Production' campaigns. The entire population of China by then was starving as a result of the communisation of agriculture, horticulture and animal husbandry, which resulted in total crop failures and massive loss of livestock, aggravated further by severe starvation-diet rationing of all foodstuffs for the entire population except for the privileged few senior Communist Party officials, the army and police force officers.

The entire Chinese economy was ruined by Chairman Mao's brainless experimentation with the communisation of agriculture, horticulture and animal husbandry, which led to the decimation of livestock numbers, aggravated further by primitive attempts at 'overtaking England's steel production' in hand-made furnaces burning coal and iron ore and producing slack instead of steel, and bird eradication campaigns aimed at decimating all birds in China supposedly to improve agricultural output, whereas everybody in China was expected to take an active part in making improvised primitive coal-fired steel smelters that ended up producing useless slack in huge quantities.

Catching and killing birds as well as mice and rats, supposedly to save crops from being eaten by them, was the official policy to be undertaken by the entire population. In reality, these idiotic actions were used as a tool to identify potential unwilling participants in order to dispatch them into labour death camps as undesirable class enemies or enemies that ignored Mao's appeals for active participation in production activities.

Even I remember as a school student how much effort I had to put in to catch a few mice as well in order to cut off their tails and legs and deliver them to school to my teachers as proof of active participation in these mouse and bird eradication campaigns.

Alongside the communisation of agriculture campaigns, the Chinese authorities were actively conducting population reduction campaigns in the cities, where any inhabitant of the city selected by the local authorities to be 'sent down' could be assigned, together with his or her entire family, to relocate to a designated agricultural commune to provide an additional workforce to support the agricultural output of that commune; that is, to help plant crops, weed and water them when needed and eventually harvest them if anything has grown, all done by hand using primitive tools and implements. It did not matter if the persons selected for 'sending down' (or *Xia Fung* in Chinese), did not have the slightest idea how to grow anything, as the main criteria for selection was to target those who were suspected of being disloyal to the communist regime, or were the owners of houses or other quality abodes coveted by the Communist Party officials or those in power in that particular location.

By evicting inhabitants of desirable abodes into the countryside agricultural communes with primitive dwellings, their houses were taken over and distributed to the Party faithful.

Those who resisted such transfer orders could be deprived of their food rations and be starved to death if they disobeyed the orders to 'move down' to the agricultural communes in the countryside, or alternatively, to be arrested and dispatched to labour 're-education' death camps.

I remember my uncle, Sayed Azrael Gabitov, being targeted for such a 'send down' transfer together with his family in order to take over his house for occupation by a senior Chinese official and his family, as his house was considered to be large and of good quality. This process involved his temporary detention into protracted 'study seminars' of Chairman Mao's 'Red Book', which could only be described as a mental and physical torture of the individuals targeted, as they had to spend long hours—often without any food or drinks—memorising and uttering aloud Chairman Mao's 'Red Book' scriptures praising the 'Red Sun' as well as the Communist Party as a loud verbal display of loyalty to Chairman Mao and his communist regime.

My uncle eventually managed to get out of it by surrendering half of his house to be occupied by a senior Chinese official. Although he ended up getting along well with the Chinese official and his family and even building up some sort of friendship with them, he, nonetheless, ended up in protracted detention in a Chinese prison without any charge. The fact that he served in 1944–1945 in the East Turkestan Army as a colonel in charge of supplies to the frontline during that war, may have played a big role in his being subjected to incessant and continuous hounding by the Chinese authorities, which somehow managed to target him in each and every ongoing re-education campaign as well as trying to dispatch him and his family into the countryside to work in an agricultural commune as a scapegoat-labourer, despite him being a highly educated person. Chairman Mao's henchmen often labelled such persons targeted for eviction from the cities into agricultural communes, '*xia fung*', to be utilised as beasts of burden there as '*huai dan*', or 'rotten eggs', when translated into English.

The Chinese economy was in a state of total collapse when in 1963, Liu Shaoqi and Deng Xiaoping decided to orchestrate a subtle coup against Mao, whereby they took over leadership of the country, especially the management of the economy, while still retaining Chairman Mao as the figurehead 'Red Sun'. Keeping Chairman Mao as the 'Red Sun' not subject to any criticism or scrutiny, turned out to be a very bad miscalculation on their part, as it ended up backfiring on them in 1966 by allowing Mao to start his 'Cultural Revolution' in order to depose them.

From 1963 onwards the Chinese economy started to recover somewhat under Deng's management, who relaxed communisation of agricultural output and allowed farmers to cultivate private plots in addition to working on the communal lands. The peasants were also allowed to sell their surplus produce privately on the free markets created outside the fixed-price rationing system, thus relaxing starvation rationing of foodstuffs to the population. As a result of these reforms implemented by Liu Shaoqi and Deng Xiaoping, from 1963–1966 the Chinese economy recovered somewhat from the brainless excesses of the Mao era.

In 1959, our mother decided to have a second go at travelling into mainland China with her five children—my eldest brother, Illhan, who was then 18 years old; brother Raiph, who was then 16; myself, then 13; my younger sister, Nailya, then 10 years old; and younger brother, Ramil, then only four. Our father, Sagit, was then imprisoned in Urumchi supposedly awaiting trial since his arrest in 1958 on concocted charges of being a foreign spy attempting to escape into a capitalist country. All my mother's petitions trying to prove his innocence and appealing for his release from so-called 'preliminary detention' were being ignored, so it was her idea to try and leave the country for Australia with her five children in order to escape the misery of an oppressed, food rationed, semi-starvation lifestyle into the free world.

Her biggest mistake was that she chose the wrong destination. Instead of going to Shanghai, where she might have succeeded in leaving for Hong Kong and then to Australia with her five children under the 'White Russian refugee intake policy'—as some Russian refugee families from Sinkiang (Xinjiang) were then succeeding in getting exit visas from the Chinese authorities in Shanghai—she decided to go to Beijing and attempt to get her entry visa to Australia.

This was a big mistake, because after her visit to the Office of the British Chargé d'Affaires in Beijing, where she did get her entry visa into Australia, the Chinese authorities arrested her and told her to go back to Xinjiang under armed escort.

Had she gone to Shanghai instead, we would have had a reasonably good chance of leaving for Hong Kong after getting exit visas from the Chinese Foreign Affairs office alongside some Russian families from Xinjiang, who had succeeded in doing so.

In late 1959 it was announced over the radio that some

'British spies and their Chinese collaborators working in the Foreign Affairs Office there' had been arrested in Shanghai. These 'British spies' turned out to be my teachers from the private British School in Shanghai I was attending together with my younger sister, Nailya, namely, Mr King, Mr John and Mr Koo, who were all British missionaries teaching at the school to earn a living in addition to their missionary work. Late autumn of 1959 was the time when Mao resorted to mass China-wide arrests of millions of people to fill up his 'labour re-education camps'. So, the British missionaries were out of place and out of time, ending up in Chinese communist prisons alongside Chinese Foreign Affairs cadres who were then regarded as 'foreign collaborators and enemies of the people' due to their well-educated backgrounds as well as knowledge of foreign languages.

To this day I do not know what eventually happened to my British school teachers; whether they got starved to death in the Chinese death camps, or British diplomats succeeded in getting them out of jail and out of China, as they were British citizens who had underestimated the brutality of Mao's communist regime through their misguided desire to do missionary work in Communist China in order to convert the Chinese to Christianity.

In late autumn of 1959, we were escorted back to the capital city of Urumchi in Xinjiang province by the Chinese guards, with a one-week midway stopover in Lanzhou. Upon our arrival in Urumchi, my mother was first kept for a few weeks in Urumchi together with my 10-year-old younger sister, Nailya, and four-year-old youngest brother, Ramil. The Chinese authorities then made a decision to separate her from her children in order to dispatch our mother to one of Mao's 'labour re-education' death camps in Central Xinjiang in the vicinity of Lake Lob Nor, or *Tsou Hu* in Chinese. *Tsou Hu Lung Chang*, when translated from Chinese, was supposed to mean 'Lob Nor Agricultural Enterprise'. In reality, it was turned into a typical death camp with some 5,000 workers who were slowly starved to death through malnutrition and hard labour while trying to grow agricultural produce by diverting water from the Tarim River not far from Lake Lob Nor in harsh, desert conditions. My mother ended up getting dispatched there as punishment in order to work there as a dentist/medical worker in a small hospital attached to the camp, which was open for the local population, the camp's management, as well as the inmates of the labour camp.

The Chinese authorities recognised the fact that she was a highly qualified dentist/medical worker with experience in treating wartime injured patients as well as patients with dental problems.

It is appropriate to mention here that during the two years she spent working in the hospital attached to the death camp she saved hundreds of inmates of this camp from certain death by tirelessly injecting them with vitamins as well as glucose intravenously. In the years that followed these tragic events, I often came across former inmates who survived, expressing deep gratitude to my mother for her efforts in saving them from certain death.

When our mother was exiled to work in the Lob Nor hospital, we did our best to support her diet by sending her hard-to-come-across, highly-priced biscuits as well as cooking oil and other non-perishable foodstuffs. This made it easier for her to survive the starvation diet prevalent in the Lob Nor death camp at the time.

Oddly enough, the last Head of Tsou Hu Lung Chang, assigned from the provincial capital of Urumchi to release surviving inmates and to oversee disbanding of the death camp—by the name of Feng Chang Jiang—somehow ended up relocating to Kuldja in the years that followed these tragic events. He sought out our family and ended up becoming more or less like a family friend, telling me that not only the camp inmates held my mother in high esteem, but also the entire leadership of the camp. He became a frequent visitor to our house, dropping in for a cup of tea now and then for a friendly discussion about the overall political and economic situation in the country. He told us that his contacts in Beijing talked about the overall relaxation of the communist dictatorship in the country, leading to the privatisation of agriculture as well as industrial production in order to accelerate economic development and improve the living standards of the population overall. He also told me that one of the key leaders visiting from the provincial capital, Urumchi—Inspector General Wang Chu Zhang—who was sent to inspect and finalise the closure of the camp, somehow ended up getting severely ill upon arrival at the camp through nervous stress, unable to sleep or even eat normal food.

The head doctor of the hospital failed to give him successful intravenous injections, so my mother was called in to administer the intravenous injections as well as to design a special diet to help him with his stomach spasm. My mother ended up boiling half a chicken and preparing special Tatar-style, hand-made spaghetti chicken soup, followed by other light chicken- and lamb-broth-based dishes. Within a week the Inspector General got well enough to resume his work.

Once back on his feet, the first order he made was to get our mother's release papers prepared in order to transfer her back to Kuldja to reunite with her children living there. He even promised to help our mother to release her husband—our father, Sagit Sadriddinov—from the central prison camp in Urumchi upon his return there. Unfortunately, he failed in his effort; telling my mother upon meeting her in Urumchi when she came to see him, that our father had already been sentenced earlier to seven years of hard labour, so it was impossible for him to overturn the sentence that had already been passed on him.

In 1960, the Chinese authorities suddenly announced that they would start granting exit visas for the Russian migrants living in Kuldja to leave for Australia directly through Hong Kong. Until then, only the Russians who succeeded in stealthily travelling to Shanghai in Central China had been allowed to get exit visas for Australia after obtaining them from the British Consulate in Shanghai. We all rushed to fill out the application forms, but naturally getting visas for us was a futile exercise, because both our parents were then still in detention. Nonetheless, after sending out a couple of hundred Russian families, selectively singling out and giving preference to dispatch the Baptist and Pentecostal Russian families, the exit visa program was abruptly halted by the local Chinese authorities. Rumour had it that the Russian diplomatic missions, still very influential in China, objected to the practice, halting it as a result.

Thus, we were left to fend for ourselves, going to the mountains 100 kilometres away, where we still had our mountain hut, to open up a small plot of land and plant potatoes, beetroot and carrots there in order not to starve ourselves on meagre corn and wheat-flour rations allowed to be purchased by us by the local Chinese authorities.

As a 15-year-old boy together with my older brother, Raiph, who was then 18, we worked hard to fend for ourselves with a harvest of close to one ton of potatoes grown in summer time and stored to consume throughout the year. Our oldest brother, Illhan, who was then 20 years old, was bedridden with tuberculosis of his hip-bone, and unable to do any physical work as a result.

Mass starvation and the resultant deaths from malnutrition of the local population in 1960–1961 forced many local Uighurs, Kazakhs, Uzbeks and other local minority groups to escape across the border into the Soviet Union. Once it became obvious that they were not getting forcibly returned by the Soviet authorities as a result of deteriorating political relations between the Soviet leadership then led by Nikita Khrushchev and Chairman Mao in China, the locals started to escape into the Soviet Union *en masse,* despite the high risk of getting shot by the Chinese border guards when attempting to cross the sparsely populated vast border region. By 1962, mass discontent caused by acute hunger and the resultant deaths from malnutrition, started to manifest itself in open defiance of the local Chinese authorities, who were trying to control the population by detaining and sending large numbers of men and women to starve and die in the numerous concentration labour camps.

On 29 May 1962, a large crowd of several thousand Uighur, Kazakh and Uzbek youths first went demonstrating in front of the 'Yili Kazakh Autonomous Region Government' headquarters in Kuldja. They then stormed into the large, three-storey building and dragged out the head of the local Kazakh Regional Government. The elderly Kazakh Regional Government head by the name of Kurban Gali, pleaded with the demonstrators not to beat him up, saying, 'Why are you mistreating me? Don't you understand that I am just a slave of the Chinese like yourselves?' to which the demonstrators retorted, 'If you are the slave of the Chinese like us, then why are you so fat, whereas all of us in front of you here are slim and severely malnourished?'

The demonstrators then decided to attack the Regional Communist Party headquarters run by the Chinese Communist Party secretary.

Frightened Chinese-speaking local Communist Party leaders had earlier summoned a detachment of armed Chinese soldiers inside the Regional Communist Party headquarters' building perimeter. Once the roaring crowd of several hundred jumped over the spiked iron fence, opened the gates and rushed towards the main three-storey building, the Chinese Communist Party secretary ordered the soldiers to open fire with their submachine guns, mowing down several hundred attacking unarmed demonstrators who had managed to enter the perimeter of the Communist Party headquarters from the outside square.

We were then at home a couple of kilometres away from the city centre, but even there we could hear several bursts of submachine gunfire accompanied by the terrifying cries of several thousands of mostly young local Uighurs, Kazakhs and Uzbeks, who took part in the demonstrations outside the Regional Government as well as the adjoining Regional Communist Party headquarters in the city centre. The survivors of the submachine gunfire naturally ran to escape the carnage. It was rumoured later that the Chinese soldiers came out into the square in front of the Communist Party headquarters, bayoneting wounded demonstrators lying down who were unable to escape, and dragging them inside together with the dead bodies. The survivors who were crowded outside all over the square ran for their lives to escape the carnage. They all headed towards the Kazakhstan border of the Soviet Union, which was close to 100 kilometres away at the Khorgos or Chapchal checkpoints, stretching over the valley across the Yili River, and then for hundreds of kilometres over the Tian Shan Mountain range. Sadly enough, for unknown reasons, the Soviet authorities sealed the border from 1 June 1962 onwards, turning back the refugees who arrived after that date.

They were then imprisoned by the Chinese authorities upon their return. The Chinese must have obviously made very strong representations to force the Soviet authorities to make that decision, despite the fact that from 1959–June 1962 several hundreds of thousands of Uighur, Kazakh, Uzbek and other ethnic minority refugees escaped across the porous border sparsely controlled by the Chinese border guards, who had stayed indoors at night to let the refugees cross the border unimpeded until the tragic massacre of 29 May 1962.

The Chinese authorities also expelled Soviet consulates from Kuldja, Chuguchak and the provincial capital of Urumchi in the second half of 1962, imprisoning locally hired employees who did not enjoy diplomatic immunity despite being Soviet citizens. Some of them ended up dying in Chinese prisons or eventually getting expelled into the Soviet Union. A couple of lucky ones—Tashmuhammed Umarov and Nael Gabitov, who happened to be loosely related to distant relatives of my extended family—were helped by me to migrate to Australia in the early 1980s.

During the artificial famine years of 1960–1963 created by Chairman Mao and his henchmen to confine into labour camps the 'undesirable elements and upper classes' of China, exterminating in the process more than 50 million people through starvation and hard labour, the entire population of China, other than the ruling elite of the Communist Party apparatus, was subjected to starvation rationing of all foodstuffs. In order to survive, we decided to go to the mountains of Talky, where we still had our log cabin built as a summertime holiday retreat. The black mountain soil not far from the cabin was ideal for planting potatoes and it was possible to irrigate the potato plants by diverting a small stream of water from the mountain rivulet flowing nearby.

At that stage the mountains were sparsely populated by nomadic Kazakhs, who were friendly to us, as the communist regime had not yet exercised firm control over the mountains. My elder brother, Raiph, and I managed to grow well over a couple of tons of high-quality potatoes over the summer months and take the crop to the city of Kuldja to be stored in a cool, underground cellar and eaten over the following months until the new crop.

We also managed to hide in the mountains and keep a couple of rifles and shotguns in our possession, which proved to be an invaluable asset in supplanting our diets by shooting mountain reindeer and mountain goats, as well as hunting for wild game. The mountains and the jungles along the Yili River were then sparsely populated and therefore not properly controlled by the Chinese authorities, so it was possible to hunt and preserve wild game meat to be consumed all year round. In early winter we would go to the jungles of the Yili River to shoot, gut out, salt inside and freeze up to 300 wild pheasants, to take them home to stew and consume with potatoes and carrots, which provided us with delicious, high-nutrition meals. I often supplanted them with wild ducks, inhabiting marshes 10–15 km outside the city of Kuldja by getting up before dawn and travelling there riding a small motorbike with a shotgun disassembled and discreetly tied up to the motorbike. I would get there by dawn and walk through the marshes in rubber boots, shoot three or four ducks to take home to cook, water boiling wild ducks with a small quantity of rice; again making a delicious duck-meat, rice-porridge meal.

All this was done in winter in addition to trying to attend high school on weekdays, as high school was held during the afternoon shift in the same building that taught primary school children in the morning shift.

Somehow, I still managed to carry on with my studies, even getting distinction marks and top student book prizes from school alongside getting recognition as the top chess champion in the city of Kuldja.

5

Liu Shaochi Era in China

By 1963, the Chinese leadership headed by Liu Shaoqi decided to sideline Chairman Mao, who failed in his ill-fated 'Great Leap Forward' and communisation of agriculture, whereby peasants were not allowed to even cook their own meals at home, but were rather forced to eat their meagre rations from the shared communal kitchens. Liu Shaoqi took over leadership of the starving country and was entrusted with the task of relaxing collective agricultural production rules by allowing peasants to toil on their individually assigned plots for their own food production in addition to working effectively free of charge on communal land. This relaxed Chairman Mao's idiotic 'Great Leap Forward' and policies of total communisation of agricultural production of the entire vast country, combined with the creation of a vast network of 'Re-education by Labour' concentration camps to detain many millions of 'the undesirable and the upper-class, (so-called rotten-egg elements'), which resulted in countrywide mass starvation in the period 1959–1962, leading to deaths from hunger and the resultant malnutrition and diseases of more than 50 million people China-wide.

To change things around for a better supply of foodstuffs, Liu Shaoqi allowed peasants access to small private plots of land to grow their own foodstuffs as well as to sell their surplus produce on the open market outside the strict food rationing regime prevalent nationwide at the time, thus gradually alleviating and ending starvation of the entire population of China.

By 1964, open agricultural markets were thriving throughout the country. Somehow, Liu Shaoqi and his comrades made a big mistake by finding it convenient for themselves to keep Chairman Mao as a national deity, instead of dismantling his status and image as a national deity alongside dismantling his idiotic policies of governance through mass imprisonment and mass starvation of the population. By 1966, the country's economy was back in reasonable shape. That is when Chairman Mao and his cohorts decided to take back power through the devious idea of a 'Cultural Revolution'.

Chairman Mao declared that he would start a 'Cultural Revolution' to remove all the vestiges of western civilisation and culture from China, denouncing by burning all books published before 1960 in China as well as books published overseas and brought into China as 'yellow books'. Chairman Mao must have learned his methods well from Hitler, as he not only detained all intellectuals who were regarded as undesirable, just like Hitler did, but also applied the ancient

Chinese practice of parading them—by dragging them in front of mass demonstrations screaming obscenities at them—with high, half-a-metre or more long paper hats traditionally reserved in ancient China for criminals convicted to the death penalty. To implement this mass 'Cultural Revolution' movement, Mao deployed the so-called 'Red Guards'—mostly young, high school and university students as well as young, unemployed scum off the streets, rather than employ traditional army or police force members. Liu Shaoqi and his cohorts initially misunderstood Mao's purpose and designs by going along with it as another whim of the 'Red Sun'.

Very soon they would discover to their own peril the true purpose of Chairman Mao's 'Cultural Revolution'. Once the 'Red Guards' armed detachments' frenzy was whipped up with millions taking part in it supposedly to round up, detain and eliminate upper- and middle-class elements of Chinese society, Chairman Mao suddenly declared that the true enemies of the 'Cultural Revolution' and of the 'Red Guards' were hiding within the Communist Party membership ranks of China. Now, instead of dragging out the intellectuals of China with their hands tied up and wearing high paper hats on their heads, they were released and left alone, grabbing instead the Communist Party functionaries, putting high paper hats on their heads and obscene placards on their bodies, dragging them out into the streets to drumbeats and fanfare as 'rotten eggs', the enemies of Chairman Mao and the enemies of the Cultural Revolution.

This was done by Mao's 'Red Guards' against the entire Chinese Communist Party's higher ranking membership nationwide, starting with Liu Shaoqi himself as well as most of the Chinese Communist Party elite. Naturally, some of the Chinese army as well as police force elements tried to oppose this wanton destruction of the ruling hierarchy, leading to total chaos and lawlessness in the vast country. This also resulted in widespread armed clashes between the warring factions supporting Mao and his 'Red Guards' on the one side, and supporters of Liu Shaoqi and his Communist Party hierarchy on the other side, leading to a few years of complete chaos and lawlessness in the country starting in 1966, then culminating in the so-called Du Pi Gai campaign of 1969–1972 (Du Zheng, Pi Pan, Gai Zou, or Struggle, Criticise and Punish, Correct and Change). This campaign not only resulted in mass beatings and physical abuse of its victims, but also numerous deaths and suicides, followed by expulsions of millions of city-dwellers out of their living abodes into the agricultural communes in the countryside. Chairman Mao's wife, Jiang Chin, together with General Lin Biao started playing important roles in the internal struggles of the Chinese Communist Party and army elite, until eventually getting themselves eliminated in 1974–76.

Photo left: Mr. Roostam Sadri, President of the Tatar Association of South Australia, giving a speech at the 2006 Adelaide Saban Tui.
Photo right: Hon. Jack Snelling MP at the 2006 Adelaide Saban Tui.

His Excellency Mr. Rustam Minnikhanov, President of Tatarstan, presenting a speech in Adelaide, 2011

His Excellency Mr. Rustam Minnikhanov, President of the Republic of Tatarstan, Hon. Jack Snelling MP and Hon. Grace Portolesi MP with members of the Tatar community in Adelaide on the 27th of September 2011.

His Excellency Mr. Rustam Minnikhanov, the President ofTatarstan, Hon.Jack Snelling MP and Hon Grace Portolesi MP are with Tatar community in Adelaide on 27 September 2011

Mr. Azrail Abid in
Adelaide, 1985.

Roostam Sadri and his daughters Camila, Zahra and Sophia with His Excellency Mr Rustam Minnikhanov, President of Tatarstan

Students of the Adelaide Tatar Ethnic School marching at the Multicultural Children's Day parade

Students of the Adelaide Tatar Ethnic School in their national costume in Adelaide in 1999

Students of the Adelaide Tatar Ethnic School at the Multicultural Children's Day Festival in Adelaide in 1992

Australian Tatar singer Zulya Kamalova receiving a letter of appreciation from His Excellency Mr. Rustam Minnikhanov, President of the Republic of Tatarstan, in Adelaide in 2011.

Kazan Dance Ensemble performing a Crimean Tatar folk dance "Bakchasaray" at the 2006 Adelaide Saban Tui.

Mr. Sagit Sadri and Mrs. Lailya Sadri with their awards from His Excellency Mr. Rustam Minnikhanov, President of the Republic of Tatarstan.

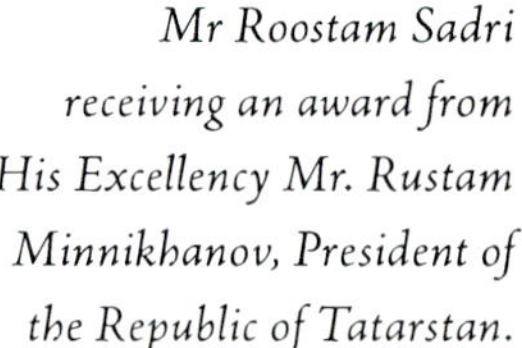

Mr Roostam Sadri receiving an award from His Excellency Mr. Rustam Minnikhanov, President of the Republic of Tatarstan.

Mr. Sagit Sadri and Mrs Lailya Sadri, taken during a visit to the Tatar community in Helsinki in 1984

Mr. Sagit Sadri and Mrs Lailya Sadri celebrating their 50th wedding anniversary in 1989.

Mr. Sagit Sadri and Mrs. Lailya Sadri celebrating their 70th wedding anniversary in Adelaide in 2009.

Members of Adelaide's Tatar community with the Hon. Michael Atkinson MP and the Hon. Lindsay Simmons MP at a reception for the 60th anniversary of Tatar settlement in South Australia at Parliament House in South Australia in February 2021.

Members of Adelaide's Tatar community in the House of Assembly chamber at Parliament House with the Hon Michael Atkinson MP.

Mr Sadri

I am pleased to hear that you are celebrating your one hundredth birthday. My sincere congratulations and best wishes on this very special day.

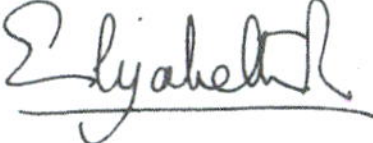

I am pleased to send you my sincere congratulations on this special occasion.

I hope that your celebration is a memorable one shared with family and friends.

With best wishes for the future.

PRIME MINISTER

Certificate of Congratulations

Mr Sagit Sadri

on the occasion of your

100th Birthday

on Saturday the 19th of August 2017

The Hon Malcolm Turnbull MP

My father, Mr Sagit Sadri was very pleased to receive a congratulatory message from her Majesty Queen Elizabeth II and a certificate of congratulations from Prime Minister Malcom Turnbull for his 100th birthday.

GOVERNMENT HOUSE, *Canberra Australia*

Dear Mr Sadri

My wife Lynne and I send you our warmest congratulations for the occasion of your one hundredth birthday.

May this very special day be a happy and memorable one.

Yours sincerely

His Excellency General the Honourable
Sir Peter Cosgrove AK MC (Retd)
Governor-General
Commonwealth of Australia

ТАТАРСТАН РЕСПУБЛИКАСЫ ПРЕЗИДЕНТЫ

Рәхмәт хаты

Хөрмәтле Сәгыйть Садри!

Көньяк Австралиянең Аделаидадагы Татар Ассоциациясенә нигез салучы буларак, туган халкыбыз мәнфәгатьләрендә күркәмле хезмәтегез, аның рухи-әхлакый һәм мәдәни традицияләрен саклап калуга һәм үстерүгә зур өлеш кертүегез өчен Сезгә ихлас рәхмәтемне җиткерәм. Зирәк акыллы, күркәмле шәхес, талантлы эшкуар һәм оештыручы – Сез Австралия татар җәмгыятендә олы абруй казандыгыз, югары гражданлык активлыгы һәм ватанпәрвәрлек үрнәге булып торасыз.

Сезгә тирән ихтирамымны белдерәм, чын күңелдән нык сәламәтлек һәм иминлек телим.

Татарстан Республикасы Президенты — **Р.Н.Миңнеханов**

Казан, Кремль, 2011 елның 15 сентябре

6

Ten Years of our Secluded Life in the Tora Su Mountains

Once it became obvious to us in 1965 that the Chinese authorities were not going to issue exit visas to our family, we decided to secure our livelihood, and so we decided to buy a small, dilapidated apiary in the Achi Gorge not far from the Tora Su Mountains from one of the last departing Russian families. The small apiary consisted of close to thirty old beehives set up next to a dugout cabin of three rooms with a plot of land in front of it to plant potatoes and other vegetables. The surrounding mountain slopes were, however, very picturesque with an abundance of wildflowers as well as delicious wild raspberries, strawberries, blackberries, wild apricots and apples growing naturally there. A cold, clean mountain stream flowing downhill next to the cabin had plenty of wild mountain trout fish, where it was easy to catch a full bucket with a net. They were delicious to eat when grilled or smoked with dry apple or apricot wood. Wild reindeer and mountain goats were also hiding in the surrounding mountain gorges. They could be hunted during the autumn/early winter hunting season and their meat could then be processed and preserved for year-round consumption.

We set out immediately to build an additional proper house and to also make new beehives in order to expand our bee farm, as there were plenty of large fir trees available for the purpose. At the same time, we planted potatoes and other vegetables such as carrots, turnips, cabbages, and the like, to be self-sufficient in all our foodstuff needs. Whatever other products we needed we could exchange for our honey, as ours was a very high-quality, aromatic, wildflower honey, in short supply for the inhabitants living down in the valley. So we had rice, wheat flour and hemp oil in exchange for our honey from the farmers in the Yili Valley.

Through hard work we gradually managed to increase the number of our beehives to 110 hives, capable of producing close to five tons of high-quality, aromatic, wildflower honey per season, the revenue from which was more than enough for us to sustain a high-quality lifestyle by local standards. We also acquired and raised a small herd of some nine cattle to be self-sufficient in butter, cheese and other milk products all year round. To sustain the cattle through the harsh winter months, we had to harvest large stacks of hay in summer. Whenever we wanted to get lamb meat to supplement our diet for a change, in addition to our preserved, lean, healthy mountain reindeer or goat meat, the local Kazakh nomads would deliver fresh lamb in exchange for our honey and potatoes.

The Tora Su Gorge and Achi Mountains surrounding our

apiary were then sparsely populated, with Kazakh nomads arriving and moving around to graze their livestock in the summer months. The mountains around our apiary would get covered in deep snow in the winter months. Just a few families of Kazakh nomads with their goats and horses would normally settle in there for the winter, as the majority would go away with their sheep, cattle and horses in order to survive the harsh winter in the Yili or Borotala Valleys, to where there was more fodder and less snow to sustain their livestock through harsh winter conditions.

This resulted in the absence of any permanent Chinese army or police presence throughout the mountain ranges. Our apiary bees would also hibernate inside their hives for over four months of harsh mountain winter, brought in after the first snowfall and stuck into a dugout shelter specially built for the purpose.

It was overall hard work to build up the bee numbers for the flowering season, to extract honey from the beehive frames full of honey during the brief 40–60-day high flowering season of June–July in the summer time. Then we had to work to prepare all the hives for the winter months by putting warm blanket insulation on top of them and making sure the hives contained enough honey for the bees to last through the winter season. We had to also cut down and store large quantities of dry firewood from the mountain slopes to last us through the winter months, as it would be difficult to harvest the firewood in deep snow during winter. At least four weeks of summer–early autumn were spent working to cut and store a few very large, freshly-dried green haystacks, making sure they would be enough to last throughout the winter for our two horses and 9–10 head of cattle. The honey produced in summer had to be moved from our bee farm on horseback by our two oxen, to be taken to the city of Kuldja and sold there, as it was in short supply and not generally available on the market. So, everybody, including the Chinese officials residing there, wanted to buy our honey for their own consumption.

Whatever foodstuffs and other necessities we needed to last us through the winter months we had to grow ourselves or procure—often in exchange for our honey—and then cart it back to our mountain retreat, using our horses and oxen before the onset of winter, as it was quite difficult to travel in the mountains even some 70–80 kilometres over the deep snow in winter months. Our lifestyle in the mountains was very healthy in terms of the pristine mountain environment, clean air and nutritious food. We were, however, under constant stress from the lawlessness and chaos that started with the onset of Chairman Mao's so-called 'Cultural Revolution' in the cities throughout China, as we still had to visit the city of Kuldja in the summer months, especially prior to the onset of severe winter conditions, when temperatures in the mountains often dropped below -20 °C. We had a good-quality, portable, short-wave transistor radio in the mountains, which was able to receive transmissions from not only the Chinese and Russian broadcasting stations, but also Voice of America,

BBC, Deutsche Welle and so on, in both English as well as Russian languages, so even when living in the mountains we were always well-informed about what was happening in China as well as overseas throughout the world.

Close to the summer of 1966, radio waves started broadcasting stories of atrocities being committed by Chairman Mao's 'Red Guards' against the intellectuals and the educated middle-class citizens in general—ransacking their homes, confiscating and burning their books in the streets as well as parading the victims in the streets with their hands tied up and wearing high paper hats inscribed with Chinese characters 'huai dan' or 'rotten egg'. Chairman Mao, himself born into a well-off, middle-class family, indulged as a student of ancient history in his younger years, so he must have remembered that this custom of parading criminals in high paper hats was traditionally reserved in ancient China for criminals condemned to the death penalty. So, Mao's 'Red Guards' were instructed to parade their victims in the streets in front of huge crowds, who were orchestrated to shout obscenities at the victims dragged out in front of them wearing high paper hats.

The 'Red Guards' then suddenly started to selectively attack and parade in high paper hats the local administration and Communist Party officials, accusing them of being the followers of Liu Shaoqi and 'remnants of the revisionist scum in positions of power'.

So we were left alone to become mere spectators alongside

the local Uighurs, Kazakhs, Uzbeks and other minority groups to watch from a distance internal communist Chinese administration and army struggles, as they ended up splitting into two hostile armed camps—presumably one side attempting to support Liu Shaoqi and his followers, and the other side trying to eliminate them and bring into absolute power Chairman Mao together with his fourth wife, Jiang Chin, and her stooges headed by the then Communist Red Army Commander, Ling Biao.

From the autumn of 1966 onwards, several years of political and civil turmoil followed, exacerbated by armed conflict between the two warring factions struggling to establish their control over the vast country. Nonetheless, in the middle of complete turmoil and lawlessness, the Chinese Secret Service remained active by monitoring the local Uighur, Kazakh, Uzbek and other non-Chinese ethnic leaders and occasionally imprisoning or just discreetly killing them under the guise of ongoing armed conflict within the country. By the end of 1969, it was obvious that the Maoist faction took the upper hand in the internal struggle. They again targeted the ethnic minority educated class, singling out all those who were regarded as the undesirable upper-class segment of the local population. The victims were forced to stand up in front of the assembled local government stooges and be subjected to prolonged verbal abuse, which quite often escalated into physical abuse.

This abuse often culminated in the expulsion of the victims to one of the so-called agricultural communes, where they were subjected to being substituted as beasts of burden, ploughing land, planting and harvesting crops—all done by hand as slave labourers—working long hours during the day regardless of weather conditions. Their reward was basically a meagre diet verging on malnutrition and no pay whatsoever. The communes offered food from communal kitchens, controlling both the quantity and quality of maize, or cornflour, and sometimes wheat flour buns, offered alongside vegetables with minimal amounts of vegetable oils or meat added to make the food more or less edible. Basic substandard accommodation with minimal heating with coal or firewood was also provided by the commune to the exiled city dwellers, often accustomed to living in their own, much better quality houses in their city. Those who resisted or did not comply with the local authority orders risked getting sent into labour concentration camps, where starvation and exhausting labour conditions took a heavy toll on the inmates, often leading to their deaths.

7

Our Missed Chance to Migrate to Australia in 1964-65

In 1964, the Chinese authorities started again to issue exit visas—to migrate to Australia—to the holders of Australian entry visas. For some reason unknown to us they singled out for preferential treatment the Russian adherents of the Pentecostal Church, the Baptists and the Old Orthodox Church known as the 'Starovery', or the adherents of the Old Russian Orthodox Church, which existed prior to the church reforms of the first Tsar, Peter the Great, who cut their beards and the long sleeves of their extended gowns.

All the adherents of these three Russian religious denominations were told to get ready to depart for Hong Kong. A few of them who were in labour camps detained earlier for the very reason of wanting to migrate to Australia or South America, were also released prior to departure. By the end of 1964, they were all on their way to Hong Kong. For some reason, the adherents of the mainstream Russian Orthodox Church as well as holders of Soviet passports were precluded from leaving Xinjiang in 1964.

I vividly remember that in 1961–62 our aunty, Doctor Shafika Sadriddinova, prior to her departure to the Soviet Union, visited us a number of times telling us to get Soviet citizenship passports, as that would help us in the future to migrate to Australia. Unfortunately, our Uncle Azrael did not quite understand the implications of that important decision and told her off, refusing the opportunity to acquire Soviet passports. He simply failed to understand that by rejecting Soviet citizenship for all of us, he rejected the opportunity to be counted by the Chinese authorities as foreign citizens and not as Chinese residents. We were not mature enough to oppose our uncle, as we were living in his house and therefore could not argue against him. So, we failed to accept her offer to get us Soviet passports prior to her departure to the Soviet Union.

In 1965, the Chinese authorities started issuing exit visas to Australia to the holders of Soviet passports along with the remaining members of the Russian Orthodox Church. As we did not have Soviet passports and were ethnic Tatars rather than adherents of the Russian Orthodox Church, our applications for exit visas were rejected for reasons unknown to us, telling us that we were now Chinese citizens because we did not repatriate to the Soviet Union and did not hold Soviet passports.

Many years later, I found out from one of the key local Chinese Foreign Office officials, Ma Yiching, that the Chinese Foreign Office in Kuldja decided to send our exit visa applications to the Tatar head of the Political Consultative Committee of Kuldja for endorsement, anticipating that he would readily endorse it, as that would open the opportunity to migrate to Australia not only to our family seeking exit visas, but to a few other Tatar families living in Kuldja at the time as well. To their great surprise, Mr Askhat Shakirov, Tatar representative of the Political Consultative Committee of Xinjiang, refused to endorse the application by claiming that Tatars in Kuldja were Chinese citizens and therefore should remain in China as one of the fifty-four ethnic groups inhabiting China, rather than allowing them to migrate to Australia. This obscene decision of his condemned our family to remain in Communist China for another ten years. I had to study Chinese to be able to communicate with Chinese officials in their own language. I had to write many petitions to the Chinese Foreign Affairs Departments in Beijing as well as in the provincial capital Urumchi, and Kuldja locally, arguing that Tatars always lived in China as former refugees and escaped there to avoid persecution from tsarist Russia or the Soviet Union, that most of them were already repatriated to the Soviet Union and therefore the remaining few Tatar families should be allowed to leave China as well, if they desired to do so. I also made a concerted effort to build a good rapport and informal friendships with the Chinese officials in charge of the local Foreign Affairs Offices in Urumchi and Kuldja in order to persuade them eventually to help us migrate to Australia.

Finally, I succeeded in that effort in the autumn of 1975, to become the first Tatar family ever to migrate from Xinjiang to Australia via Hong Kong in December of that year.

The foreign office officials even went to the trouble of visiting our family living and working on our bee farm in the secluded mountains of Tora Su to formally notify us of their decision to issue us with exit visas to Hong Kong, so that we could conduct the orderly sale of our bee farm and other assets and get ready for departure in the next couple of months. By the end of November 1975, we boarded a bus to the provincial capital of Urumchi accompanied by two foreign office officials in order to make a train trip to Hong Kong with our suitcases full of our clothing and other household items. We were then politely sent off across the border into Hong Kong, arriving there on Christmas Eve.

In Hong Kong our family was met by the officials of the Migration Office of the World Council of Churches, who assisted us with undertaking health checks and filling out applications for entry visas into Australia as required by the condition of our preliminary approval to migrate to Australia. We found a furnished apartment to stay in until our entry visas were processed. Finally, after two months of waiting, we were told to buy our tickets to fly to Australia on a Qantas Airways flight from Hong Kong, arriving in Adelaide via Melbourne on the morning of 11 February 1976.

At the Adelaide airport our family was met by a large crowd of our Russian friends, who were allowed to migrate to Australia in the 1960s by the Chinese authorities and who were often helped by me and other members of our family with filling in their application forms for Australian visas, as we were then the one family in Kuldja who were able to read and write in English, as all letters and application forms had to be then filled in and sent to the British Consulate in Shanghai in English.

Our Russian friends even rented a house for us to live in until we found and bought our own home after securing a bank loan six months later.

After two days of resting and partying, I asked one of my friends where I could get work. He promptly suggested that I should apply for a job at a General Motors Holden's automobile plant in Woodville, which was located some four kilometres away from our rented house in the Adelaide suburb of Rosewater. I went to the address given to me and at the gate of the plant was told to go to the personnel office and fill in an application form. The personnel officer in charge, having read my application, said to me, 'You seem to have an excellent command of English and have indicated in your form that you speak several other languages as well. Are you sure you want to work on the assembly line of our plant?' I replied to him that I arrived in Australia three days ago and needed a job to earn my living. He told me then that I could start working the next day at 8 am.

The following morning, I turned up at work exactly on time and was shown to the large assembly line where I would operate a press to install seals into the automatic transmissions of Holden vehicles, which were getting assembled at the plant. I had no difficulty operating the press and was told by the foreman not to rush and just keep pace with other workers on the line after pressing each seal into position. I found the work to be somewhat monotonous, but easy to do. A couple of weeks later, the foreman told me that they needed someone on the assembly line to attach hydraulic transmissions to the engines. This task turned out to be more complicated, but I managed to learn and do it without much difficulty as well. I was pleasantly surprised that the $220 I was then earning per week could buy a lot of things. I went to an auction and bought a perfectly working ex-postal Vespa scooter for $80 to ride to work. Petrol for the scooter cost only .13 cents per litre. I also enrolled in evening courses to prepare myself to sit for the university entrance examination. Very soon I discovered that riding a scooter in heavy traffic was dangerous, to say the least, as motorists always paid attention to other cars on the road, but not to a scooter rider amongst them. So, I decided to buy a car to travel to work as well as to go around town attending evening courses and so on. I bought a second-hand Ford Cortina sedan in perfect running condition for $400 at a car auction and sold my Vespa scooter for $100 after cleaning and polishing it up to make it attractive for a potential buyer, as it was in good running condition.

Six months after starting my work at General Motors, it was suddenly announced that the Motor Workers Union was going on strike, stopping work at the Woodville plant. I told management that I needed to earn my living wages and therefore did not want to go on strike. I was then told that nobody was allowed to work at the plant when the strike was on, so I should look for casual work elsewhere while the strike was on. Disappointed, I decided to go around building sites at nearby West Lakes, not far from home, looking for casual work. There, I met a bricklayer working alone, who told me that he needed a labourer to help him to mix mortar and spread out bricks from pallets ready to be laid by him. If I worked hard for him as a labourer, he would pay me $50 per day and allow me to lay bricks on internal walls as well, as they would be plastered afterwards to cover imperfections. I saw this as an opportunity not only to earn $250 per week doing hard, physical work, but also to become a qualified bricklayer in my own right, earning more than $100 per day laying bricks.

Two weeks later, I received a message telling me to come back to work the following morning at the General Motors Woodville plant, as the strike was over. I went to the plant the following morning to tell my foreman that I was not coming back to work at the plant because I had found alternative employment elsewhere while the strike was on. The foreman told me that I was deemed to be a hard worker by the management, fit to become a foreman at the plant in the future if I continued to work there. I thanked him for all the training given to me at the plant, but said that it suited me better to work as a builder's labourer five days a week during the day, rather than shift work at the plant doing various assembly tasks, because I was soon going to sit an entrance examination at the University of Adelaide to commence full-time university studies the next year in early March 1977 if I managed to pass the mature entry exams. He wished me good luck and told me that my employment termination papers would be posted to me.

Thus, I terminated my employment with the General Motors Woodville plant in September 1976 and became a full-time bricklayer's labourer for the next three months, working hard, long hours in the summer heat alongside my bricklayer boss and at the same time laying internal wall bricks. In January 1977, I passed Adelaide University's mature entry exam and was told to enrol at the university to commence studies as a mature student. Two university professors told me during the interview that I had a choice of enrolling into the law, economics, or arts degree faculties. They were somewhat surprised to hear my choice of the Arts faculty, saying that they were expecting me to choose law degree studies, as it was usually very hard to gain access to the Law faculty. I told them that I wanted to study to become proficient in writing a book about my experiences living in Communist China, rather than becoming a lawyer who lives off earning money from dealing with other people's conflicts. They smiled and told me they respected my choice, wishing me good luck with my studies.

Once I commenced my studies at the Arts faculty of the

University of Adelaide, I chose Linguistics, Social Economics, History and Chinese Language as my first-year subjects, as I knew Chinese reasonably well. This choice left me with enough time to start teaching Russian Language at the weekend Russian Molokan community classes. I also passed examinations to become a part-time contract interpreter/translator for both the Russian and Chinese languages in addition to my full-time university studies. Mrs Jill Blewett was then Officer-in-Charge of the Interpreter Service of the Department of Immigration. She told me that the 1977 International Beekeepers' Conference would be held in Adelaide and there was a requirement to assign a simultaneous interpreter for the visiting Russian Beekeepers' delegation. All applicants for the well-paid two weeks' interpreting work had to undertake tape-recorded simultaneous test sessions, to be assessed by independent Russian/English language experts without knowing the identity of the individuals undertaking the test sessions. I was not surprised to find out that my test tape received the top mark, as my ten-year beekeeping work experience back in China undoubtedly reflected my knowledge of the subject matter. So, I ended up getting the job, which also involved time with the Russian delegation members dining out and showing them Adelaide attractions such as the South Australian Museum and Art Gallery on North Terrace as well as Cleland National Park that has Australian flora and fauna. It was quite an eye-opening experience for the members of the Russian delegation, who came out from behind the Iron

Curtain of the Soviet Union, which in 1977 was still a closed society to the outside free world.

I managed to complete my first-year studies at the University of Adelaide in 1977 with one distinction and three credits to proceed further with my studies.

Furthermore, two weeks of working with the Russian delegation as a simultaneous interpreter gave me a number of valuable contacts in the relevant Australian Government circles.

I ended up getting contract work with the Department of Immigration and Ethnic Affairs on an ongoing basis. This work supplemented my student income for four years during my full-time studies at the University of Adelaide. I succeeded in completing my Arts degree course in 1980 with Honours, majoring in Russian history, Economics and Applied Linguistics. All these four years—from 1977 until the end of 1980—I continued to work during summer vacation times as a bricklayer as well to supplement my income from working as a part-time contract interpreter/translator and a teacher of the Russian language in order to be completely self-sufficient for all my living and studying expenses.

At the same time, from 1977 onwards, I became involved in our community affairs, mostly to support my parents, Sagit and Lailya Sadriddinov, in their endeavour to organise sponsorships and to bring into Australia remnants of our Tatar community suffering from Chinese communist persecution in China together with some Uzbek and Uighur families in similar circumstances. I ended up getting elected as Honorary

President of the Islamic Society of South Australia and did a substantial amount of voluntary community work in addition to my day-to-day studies and paid work as well.

The honours degree from the University of Adelaide, which I got awarded in 1980, and a recommendation from Professor Hugh Stretton—who was my Honours Degree supervisor—gave me an opportunity to enrol in an MBA course at the prestigious Australian Graduate School of Management in Sydney and to secure a Commonwealth Postgraduate Award to complete the two-year MBA course, comprising of 16 units of study, by concentrating on studies without the need to work to sustain my living expenses.

Halfway through my MBA studies I was approached by the United States-funded Central Research of Radio Free Europe/Radio Liberty (RFE/RL) to work with them as a Senior Research Analyst, Grade GS-12. The fact that I spoke fluent Russian, Tatar and Kazakh languages in addition to my excellent knowledge of English, and the fact that I sent them a copy of my Honours thesis on Soviet Expansion in Central Asia in the 1930s and 1940s, must have played an important role in me getting this job offer. I also visited Radio Free Europe headquarters in Munich, West Germany, at the end of 1980 prior to commencing my MBA studies at the Australian Graduate School of Management (AGSM) of the University of NSW in Sydney and must have made a favourable impression on the senior personnel working there.

Five days after passing my last examination at the AGSM, I

was on a plane heading to Munich, as my new employer, Radio Free Europe, paid me my relocation expenses in advance.

On the way to Munich, I decided to stop overnight in Jeddah, Saudi Arabia, to visit Dr Ali Kettani, Director of the Islamic Foundation for Science and Technology, as he had also offered me a job to work with him at his Foundation. I was met at the Jeddah airport by a member of his staff, who took me through the security at the airport and straight into Dr Kettani's office to have a friendly conversation with him about the work being undertaken by the Foundation in Saudi Arabia. The following morning, I made a brief visit to Mecca before catching a flight to Munich. Upon arrival at the Munich airport, I was met by a member of the Radio Liberty staff, who took me to the Hilton Hotel situated close to Radio Liberty headquarters in Munich. The following morning, I was brought into the Radio Liberty premises to take a tour of the premises and commence induction procedures for my new work as a Senior Research Analyst, Grade GS-12, as I could speak several languages used at Radio Free Europe in addition to my Honours Degree in Russian History and Master's Degree in Business Administration. During the induction process, I was told not to take the same route on the way to work, or on the way back home from work as a precautionary measure, and to always park my car in a secure location. I also noticed that at the gate the security personnel carefully checked underneath and around every car entering the perimeter at the heavily guarded gate to make sure that there was not a hidden bomb that had been planted there.

I was surprised to see that the front of the Radio Liberty building facing the street was demolished by an explosion. The security personnel told me that this was the night-time work of the Baader Meinhof gang a few days earlier, prior to my arrival, which wounded a couple of security guards who were working at the time.

By then I was already transferred from the Hilton Hotel into a fully furnished apartment at a prestigious location close to the centre of Munich. Once the induction process was over, I eagerly started to do my new work. To me, the position of a Senior Research Analyst stipulated that I was supposed to support the work of individual language desks by offering them research articles that could be used for their everyday broadcasting work to the Soviet Union, which was then broadcast in 15 languages. We, as research analysts of the Central Research at RFE/RL, had access to a vast library of various official publications from the Soviet Union as well as the so-called 'samizdat' publications from dissident sources somehow dispatched through various channels into our library. All I had to do was to ask individual Tatar, Kazakh, Uzbek, Ukrainian or Russian desks which topics were of interest for them to be used in their everyday broadcasting. As I spent the previous two years churning out a vast amount of written material under pressure during my MBA research studies, I started working hard, long hours trying to be equally productive in offering research papers for the broadcasting desks. Then, one of my senior colleagues at Central Research told me to slow down and try to write research papers that would be of greater interest to the members of the United States Congress as well, rather than concentrating on work for the research desks at Radio Liberty. This came as a complete surprise to me, as I was under the impression that our main task was to support the broadcasting desks with our research work. Nonetheless, I eagerly carried on with my work. The Radio premises at the so-called Englischer Garten in Munich not only had a vast library, but also an excellent restaurant on the premises with tasty German-style dishes that were obviously subsidised by the management of the premises. I was also issued the United States Army officer's military privileges card, which gave me access to the United States Army Recreation and Training Facilities in West Germany at the time. So, there were plenty of things to do outside of working hours. I took a liking to the Olympic Stadium swimming facilities in Munich, which were not very far from my living quarters and offered an Olympic-size, heated swimming pool as well as other excellent sports and recreational facilities.

In summertime, the lakes and forests around Munich offered picturesque recreational facilities as well, whereas in wintertime mountains around Munich had excellent skiing facilities with lifts. Austria was slightly over 100 kilometres away from Munich and also offered excellent recreational facilities over its mountain ranges as well as restaurants and recreational facilities in Salzburg, located not far from the border with Germany, which was always open to free travel for cars with German number plates.

The working environment at Radio Liberty was, however, tainted by the negative aura emanating from the Soviet Union, as its propaganda machine in those times of the so-called 'Cold War' depicted it as the 'nest of CIA spies' whose broadcasts into the Soviet Union in 15 languages were then diligently blocked by the Soviet jamming stations to stop the listeners in the Soviet Union enjoying listening to them as an alternative source of truthful information emanating from the West.

During my first year of diligent work there, I published some 38 short research papers in the Radio Liberty Research Bulletin, which were often used by the broadcasting desks as source material for their broadcasts, with some Congressmen in the United States also asking for and receiving copies for their own reading as a source material about events taking place in the Soviet Union at the time.

In the meantime, I kept receiving messages from Dr Ali Kettani—Managing Director of the 'Islamic Foundation for Research and Development' attached to the World Congress of Muslim countries in Jeddah, Saudi Arabia, incorporating some 42 Islamic states—appealing to my sense of loyalty to Islamic values, and to come to Jeddah and work with him to further his cause. I found it difficult to keep refusing his appeals, as after our arrival in Australia from Communist China in 1976, I met Dr Kettani in Adelaide in 1977–78, who was a frequent visitor to Australia in those times.

Overall, my parents' tireless efforts of over more than a decade after our own arrival in Australia from Xinjiang in February 1976, resulted in the resettlement into Australia of a few hundred Tatar, Uzbek and Uighur families from Xinjiang to live comfortable lives. This was also helped by the fact that in 1977 I made a detailed submission to the Department of Immigration and Ethnic Affairs in Australia about their plight in Xinjiang under Chinese communist oppression, resulting in favourable outcomes for their entry visa applications to resettle into Australia as refugees.

Eventually, at the end of 1984, I felt compelled to succumb to Dr Kettani's appeals and decided to resign from my position as Senior Research Analyst Grade GS-12 with Radio Liberty and to go to Saudi Arabia to work with Dr Ali Kettani at his Islamic Foundation for Science, Technology and Development. Having made up my mind to leave Munich for Saudi Arabia, I applied for and obtained an honourable discharge from the Central Research of RFE/RL and, after a brief holiday in Australia, travelled to Jeddah, Saudi Arabia.

Once I arrived in Jeddah, I was met at the airport by a member of Dr Kettani's staff and whisked away through Saudi security at the airport. The next day I was issued with a diplomatic pass as an employee of the Organisation of Islamic Congress in Jeddah, Saudi Arabia, which was then a representative body for 42 Islamic states based in that city, which entitled me to travel throughout Saudi Arabia, including Mecca, without any restrictions, despite the fact that access to Mecca was then off-limits for foreigners other than at hajj times. I settled into a luxury one-bedroom apartment, bought a car and got diplomatic number plates for it, which in those days in Saudi Arabia offered added protection, because car traffic on the roads in Saudi Arabia was rather chaotic and more-or-less ruled by the 'law of the jungle', but a car with diplomatic number plates entitled the occupants of the car to get extra respect by both the Saudi police as well as other car drivers on the road.

In terms of working at the Islamic Foundation, I discovered that I had to generate work myself. So, I ended up buying IBM PCs, which were then newly produced, and organising and conducting computer training courses for the personnel of the Organisation of Islamic Congress. Afterwards, I embarked on the task of writing various articles and publishing them in the English Saudi Arabia newspaper. I remember writing three quite large articles on the plight of the Crimean Tatars in the Soviet Union, who were getting continuously mistreated and denied permission to return to their former homes in Crimea at the time. I also published, with the help of Professor Abedin, in the Middle Eastern Studies publication in London my 80-page research work titled *'Soviet Expansion in East Turkestan 1944–49'*, which was widely acclaimed then and even now gets occasionally cited as a unique research work on Eastern Turkestan, or Xinjiang Uighur Autonomous Region (XUAR), as it is called now.

East Turkestan in reality became an enslaved ethnic minority region of China incorporating almost one-fifth of its overall territory populated mostly by thirteen ethnic Muslim minority groups—Uighurs, Kazakhs, Uzbeks, Kirghiz, Turkmen, Salar and other minority groups. Under the Xi Jinping regime they have become an enslaved labour source to further his expansionist dreams as well as an abundant supply source of human body parts by way of the utilisation of political prisoners for the purpose sourced from amongst more than 2 million inmates locked up in those death camps.

Whilst residing and working in Saudi Arabia, I was very proud to organise a hajj to Mecca for my parents, Sagit and Lailya Sadriddinov, to come to Jeddah from Australia. I met them at the airport and took them home to rest and recuperate from their long trip. Then I organised three seats on a hajj-bound air-conditioned bus for the diplomatic personnel of the Organisation of Islamic Congress and we made our pilgrimage, the three of us staying overnight at Mount Arafat in an air-conditioned tent and performing all other hajj rituals in relative comfort as far as possible in those overcrowded conditions. After the hajj I took them to Medina to visit the mosque where Prophet Muhammad PBUH was buried. Then I saw them off using the diplomatic departure lounge to bypass bureaucratic Saudi departure channels, thus avoiding long departure queues at the airport at post-hajj departure times.

After working with Dr Ali Kettani for one year, as I was employed on a one-year renewable contract, I decided to leave the rather stifling living environment of Saudi Arabia and go back to Australia at the end of 1985. In Australia, I applied for and secured work as a contract research analyst with a stockbroking house, Norths. At the same time, I undertook consultancy work with Special Broadcasting Service (SBS) Australia. The then Administration Manager of SBS, Mr Nazarov, engaged me to set up a computerised payment system for the SBS personnel using Open Access accounting software, which was then a very popular software program running on IBM PC/ATs. Mr Nazarov offered me very well-paid hourly rates as a computer consultant not only to set up the SBS payment system, but also to train the accounting personnel at SBS how to use it efficiently. After accomplishing this work, in early 1987, I decided to go to the Soviet Union to explore the changing political environment during President Gorbachev's perestroika (reform), as well as to explore emerging new business opportunities in the country. Not to go empty-handed, I decided to take a few IBM/AT clones, as they were in high demand in the Soviet Union at the time due to CoCOM (arms embargo) restrictions on the supply of computers to the communist country. I had to obtain a special export permit from Australian authorities to take them with me to Russia. This gave me an opportunity to meet with a few fairly high-ranking state officials in Moscow, meeting even the then-sitting Minister of Education of the Russian Federation, Mr Saburov.

The computers were demanded and purchased by the Soviet centralised body called ELORG (Electronorgtechnica or Ministry of Software and Hardware), which in turn distributed them to various organisations within their system. On one such delivery occasion, I was taking to Moscow ten newly-produced portable notebook computers assembled in Singapore. I bought a first-class ticket to board Aeroflot's largest IL-86 jetliner, carrying with me the notebooks in my hand luggage. The IL-86 was carrying more than three hundred passengers and stopped in New Delhi for refuelling on the way to Moscow. We were told to disembark into the transit lounge while refuelling was taking place. When I tried to take my heavy hand luggage with me, Aeroflot's manager in New Delhi, Mr Petuhov, told me politely that I should leave the hand luggage on board the aircraft rather than carrying it through security scanners, assuring me that he would be on board during refuelling and therefore it would be safe to leave my hand luggage there.

As we were sitting in the transit lounge waiting to be called back after refuelling, it was announced that the replacement crew was running half an hour late, so we had to wait a bit longer before re-boarding the aircraft. Shortly after that announcement, an Indian Boeing 727 aircraft with only a crew on board, who were getting trained, overshot the runway whilst attempting to land and crashed into our fully refuelled IL-86 aircraft. This collision resulted in an enormous explosion close to the transit lounge where we were still sitting waiting to be called aboard. The concrete walls of the transit lounge did not shatter, although the explosion of the fuel shook the building, creating a huge, mushroom-like black cloud over the airport. We learned immediately after the explosion that Mr Petuhov and three other staff members refuelling the aircraft perished in the explosion alongside the crew of the Indian aircraft that caused the explosion. The Russian replacement crew was not yet on board the aircraft, so they were lucky to survive the explosion alongside the crew they were supposed to replace, as the retiring crew too had already left the aircraft. Thus, perished in the fireball was only Mr Petuhov, who had assured me that my luggage would be safe, along with three Indian workers who had just re-fuelled the IL-86 aircraft and were conducting a routine technical inspection of the undercarriage, which was mandatory prior to the aircraft's take-off authorisation.

This shock reverberated through the airport, so our stay in the transit lounge dragged on until airport personnel told us all—the three hundred-plus passengers—that a five-star hotel had been booked for us until a replacement IL-86 aircraft arrived from Moscow for us all to resume our journey. Somehow, we were forced to stay in the hotel for two nights before the replacement aircraft did arrive to take us to Moscow. All my winter clothes and personal belongings that were left on board the aircraft perished alongside the ten notebooks, leaving me out-of-pocket by more than $60,000. Upon arrival in Moscow, I lodged a claim with Aeroflot, but did not get paid a single penny by way of compensation. As I did not even have warm winter clothes to wear—this was from my memory of February 1989—I had to book a return flight and quickly returned to Australia. The Aeroflot personnel consoled us by saying that we were lucky to survive because if the replacement crew had arrived on time 30 minutes earlier, we would have all been aboard the aircraft when the explosion took place, getting killed in the fireball.

After this episode, I decided to diversify into other trading activities and went to Kazan in 1990, where I met with the President of Tatarstan, the Honourable Mr Mintimer Shaimiev, as well as his chief of staff, the Honourable Mr Haliaf Nizamov, who was introduced to me as the second most important person in the Republic of Tatarstan after Mr Shaimiev. I invited them both to visit our Tatar community in Australia.

Mr Nizamov accepted my invitation, so I organised for him a VIP visitor's visa to Australia as well as a return business class ticket on Qantas Airlines, Australia's national carrier. In Australia, the entire Tatar community gave Mr Nizamov VIP treatment, hosting a number of functions on his behalf. I also introduced him to the officials of the State Government of South Australia.

Upon his return from Australia, Mr Nizamov spoke to the President of Tatarstan and they decided to ask me to represent the Republic of Tatarstan in Australia as Honorary Plenipotentiary Representative in order to promote trading and cultural links between Australia and Tatarstan within the framework of Tatarstan being the Autonomous Republic of the Russian Federation. I opened the representative office of the Republic of Tatarstan in my newly renovated building in a prestigious location on Melbourne Street, North Adelaide, at my own cost.

The Government of the Republic of Tatarstan then decided to send a large delegation of 82 key Tatarstan government and business leaders headed by President Mintimer Shaimiev on Tatarstan's Boeing 727 aircraft at the beginning of 1996. Somehow, at the last stages of the preparation work, President Shaimiev was talked out of heading the delegation and remained in Tatarstan. So, he delegated the trip to the then Prime Minister, Farid Mukhametshin. The three-day visit ended up being hosted by the then South Australian Premier, Dean Brown, and other state government officials. During the visit, the Prime Minister of Tatarstan was shown the premises of the South Australian Meat Corporation at Gepps Cross and was told that this was the second largest meat export abattoir in Australia then owned by the State Government and that the State Government was considering its sale to the highest bidder. The Prime Minister expressed interest in the acquisition of the abattoir, as Tatarstan needed to import meat as well as tallow on an ongoing basis, as tallow then was needed in Tatarstan not only to produce soap, but also to produce glycerin, which was then processed into nitroglycerin needed for the production of solid rocket fuel as well as gunpowder, both regarded as strategically important. I was asked to negotiate its sale terms and conditions after the delegation went back to Tatarstan. As requested, I did a thorough investigation of the abattoir's operations, assets and liabilities only to discover that it was employing more than 300 workers and running at a loss of $3 million to $5 million per annum, because more than half of its workforce was either receiving disabled workers' compensation, doing light duties, or engaged in maintenance work of the equipment and facilities at the abattoir. I could see that 100 workers would be able to not only process the same number of animals, but even increase the output of meat and tallow for export if properly organised.

The State Government of South Australia advertised for expressions of interest for the acquisition of the South Australian Meat Corporation (SAMCOR) abattoir in the middle of 1996. As I was under the impression that the leadership of the Republic of Tatarstan was genuinely interested in the acquisition of the abattoir, I lodged a bid to purchase all the assets of the abattoir for $4.8 million. As there were no other viable bids on the table, the State Government decided to accept my bid. To my surprise, a message came back to me that the Republic of Tatarstan could not proceed with the acquisition because the central government in

Moscow prohibited Tatarstan to make investments overseas in Australia. So, I had to make the decision either to proceed with the acquisition of the abattoir in my own right as a high-risk business venture, or to apologise on behalf of the Tatarstan Government and withdraw the acquisition offer. The State Government of South Australia had earlier produced a detailed valuation of the land, buildings, equipment and all other assets of the abattoir for $17 million. So, acceptance of the offer for $4.8 million was motivated by the fact that the abattoir business was losing between $3 million to $5 million annually to the State Government of South Australia. That is why no other meat processing business was interested in risking the acquisition of such a high-risk, loss-making venture.

Before making the offer of $4.8 million I did an in-depth evaluation of the operations of SAMCOR and was surprised to discover that out of 312 full-time paid employees, 42 were receiving permanent workers' compensation payments, 72 were on light duties (that is doing virtually no productive work) and 65 employees were either maintenance tradesmen or staff performing administrative duties. This left only 133 workers to do actual meat processing work or to operate the offal rendering plant to produce tallow as well as meat-and-bone meal to be used as a fodder additive, or as a high-potency fertiliser. This setup virtually locked in a permanent loss-making modus operandi for SAMCOR. Management incompetence was also a factor, as a large amount of clean, hot water was dumped into the stormwater drains at the rendering plant instead of pumping it to water storage tanks to be utilised for washing processing equipment in the main plant after each shift. Instead of using freely available hot water from the rendering plant, metered, costly town water was heated up by electric heaters and then was used for washing plant and equipment on a daily basis after each and every shift, resulting in annual water and electricity consumption bills in excess of $900,000. When I questioned the rationale behind this wasteful modus operandi, I was told there were no stainless-steel tanks available to pump and store hot water from the rendering plant and that as SA Water and Electricity Trust were also State Government-owned operations similar to SAMCOR, money was getting paid and transferred within the same State Government departments, so it did not really matter even if it looked like a huge loss-making enterprise for the State Government.

I could see that SAMCOR could be turned around and made into a reasonably profitable export meat processing operation if productivity was drastically improved. So, I made it a condition of purchase that the State Government would terminate the employment of all 312 workers and pay them out all their termination payments. I would then buy only the 48 hectares of land as well as plant and equipment for $4.8 million and employ close to 100 workers who were actually capable of doing proper meat processing work. The State Government had to accept the terms and conditions of my offer, as there were no other offers available to them. The State Government ended up doing well in the end, as I had to pay an additional

$300,000 plus stamp duty as well as close to $900,000 for accumulated stock in hand as well as for auxiliary plant and equipment such as trucks, earthmoving equipment and so on, bringing the total acquisition cost close to $6 million.

This meant that I had to borrow $5 million for the acquisition, as I had only $1 million of my own money saved from more than ten years of working overseas. The $17 million official valuation of SAMCOR provided by the State Government was a saving grace, as I persuaded a friendly South Australian bank manager to lend me $5 million against the $17 million valuation of the 48 hectares of land, as well as the abattoir buildings, plant and equipment, located within 10 kilometres of the Adelaide Central Business District. Once the settlement and transfer of the abattoir business to me took place in December 1996, I had no difficulty in exporting and selling close to $1 million worth of stock in hand (mostly processed frozen meat packaged for export and tallow) and using it as working capital for the initial stages of operation of the meatworks. I ended up offering employment to members of the Tatar, Uzbek and Uighur communities in Adelaide willing and able to work in the abattoir, as a large proportion of the export meat output was sent to Middle Eastern countries as halal meat, or meat suitable for consumption in those countries.

Once the plant started operating at full capacity with 102 employees, I was approached by T & R Pastoral. Its Managing Director, Darren Thomas, offered an ongoing business opportunity to buy and process cattle livestock for export as well as processing cattle supplied by them on an ongoing contractual basis. Once a successful business partnership was established, T & R Pastoral offered me sheep meat processing for export as well. In order not to overextend workforce numbers, I offered them a lease of two sheep processing lines as well as packaging and freezer facilities on an ongoing basis, which meant that SAMCOR—as it was known in the meat industry—would run under my ownership and management with guaranteed positive cash flow, rather than running at a considerable loss under the South Australian Government ownership as in the past. I also signed up ongoing contracts to supply frozen beef and tallow to Tatarstan. This business continued to operate successfully until 1999 when I decided to close the abattoir operation and start the development and sale of the real estate assets of SAMCOR. By then, in 1999, the Tatarstan market for tallow and frozen meat had collapsed due to the nearly tenfold devaluation of the Russian ruble.

T & R Pastoral acquired Metro Meat Works at Murray Bridge and notified me about their intention to quit my SAMCOR facilities at Gepps Cross. So, I had no choice but to close the abattoir operation before it started to make operating losses as a result of the departure of T & R Pastoral.

The substantial increase in land values over the three years in question from 1996–1999 was a saving grace, as I managed to sell all the abattoir plant and equipment as well as one-third of the land holdings and repay all my taxes, personnel termination liabilities and debts with the revenues derived from the sale. I ended up even getting a letter of appreciation from the Meat Workers' Union post-closure of the abattoir operations at Gepps Cross.

In 1999, the President of Tatarstan invited South Australian Premier Dean Brown to Tatarstan. As Premier Brown was not available, the official visit at the invitation of the Tatarstan Government was delegated to South Australian Deputy Premier Rob Kerin. The Australian Trade Commissioner and I met him at the Sheremetyevo Two Airport and accompanied him on board a small VIP YAK-40 jet, chartered for the Australian delegation, to Vnukovo Airport. There we were joined by the Australian Ambassador to Russia and all five of us, including Deputy Premier Kerin's ministerial adviser, flew to Kazan Airport as the visiting Australian delegation. At Kazan Airport we were met by the Tatarstan Government officials and taken to a reception given by President Mintimer Shaimiev and Prime Minister Farid Mukhametshin. During the next three days, the Australian delegation had an enjoyable time visiting the helicopter plant, getting entertained in the evenings with specially arranged concerts, and getting flown around in a Tatarstan Government VIP helicopter to visit Tatarstan countryside businesses and attractions. On the third evening, the same private VIP jet took us back to Moscow and I farewelled Vice Premier Kerin at the VIP Lounge at Sheremetyevo Two Airport.

In the year 2000, I was invited to an International Conference on Human Rights in Warsaw, Poland—in my capacity as the Plenipotentiary Representative of the Republic of Tatarstan—as President Shaimiev and Prime Minister Mukhametshin declined to attend the conference. I was surprised to discover that the high-profile conference was also attended by such high-ranking luminaries as Kofi Annan, former Secretary General of the United Nations, Madeleine Albright, former Secretary of State of the United States, former Russian Foreign Minister Igor Ivanov, the Polish Prime Minister, the Malaysian Prime Minister's delegation, some South American ministers and several other luminaries such as billionaire George Soros and so on. On the first day of the conference, I was approached by the former Russian Duma Representative on Human Rights, Mr Sergei Kovalyov, who asked me to prepare a submission in English condemning the second war in Chechnya, which was started by Vladimir Putin after five explosions in apartment buildings in Buynaksk, Moscow and Volgodonsk. These five large apartment buildings were blown up in September 1999, resulting in 307 residents' deaths as well as injuries to more than 1,000 persons living in the buildings. Vladimir Putin—then newly appointed Prime Minister by ailing President Yeltsin—blamed the Chechens despite available credible evidence that it was the Russian Federal Security Service (FSB) that organised the explosions, most likely plotted and ordered by Vladimir Putin himself. These residential apartment explosions spread a wave of fear in Russia and provided a legitimate excuse for

Putin to start the Second Chechen War in the aftermath of these explosions. The Second Chechen War catapulted Putin into the Presidency of Russia with the overwhelming help of Yeltsin's extended family, who wanted Putin to replace ailing, old drunkard Yeltsin as the new President of Russia in the hope that Putin would not touch their newly acquired immense wealth.

It is appropriate to explain here, that when the Soviet Union disintegrated in 1991 into 15 separate republics, Soviet Air Force General of Chechen background, Dzhokhar Dudayev, was elected President of Chechnya by the vast majority of the population. General Dudayev then promptly announced that Chechnya had also decided to secede from the Russian Federation and become an independent republic of Ichkeria. As Russian President Boris Yeltsin at first hesitated to wage a full-scale war against the Chechen separatists, the conflict in Chechnya dragged on until a full-scale war began in 1994, resulting in more than 100,000 lives being lost in Chechnya overall, mostly Chechen as well as Russian civilians, including combatants on both sides. This war ended on 30 August 1996 with the Khasavyurt Accord reached between the Russian General Alexander Lebed and Chechen General Aslan Maskhadov, who replaced President Dzhokhar Dudayev after his assassination on 21 April 1996. This agreement resulted in the complete withdrawal of Russian troops from Chechnya.

It should also be mentioned here that popular General Alexander Lebed ended up dead on 28 April 2002 in a mysterious helicopter crash in Abakan, as at the time he represented a real alternative to Putin to become a popular President of Russia. Chechen General Aslan Maskhadov, on the other hand, who was Chechnya's President from 1996 to 2000, was killed by the Russian FSB 'Alpha' forces on 8 March 2005 in the Chechen village of Tolstoy-Yurt.

My written submission distributed to all participants in the conference caused quite a stir, with Russian Foreign Minister Igor Ivanov walking out and never coming back to the conference again. The representative of Chechnya came to me to express his sincere gratitude, saying that they were deeply grateful to the Tatar people and to the President of Tatarstan, Mr Mintimer Shaimiev, personally for all his continuous efforts to stop the bloodshed in Chechnya.

Years later I found out that the President of the self-proclaimed independent republic of Ichkeria, General Dzhokhar Dudayev, had been killed on 21 April 1996 by a Russian long-range rocket that targeted the satellite phone signal in the hands of General Dudayev when, still hiding in the mountains near Grozny, he was talking on the phone with President Shaimiev.

The President of Tatarstan, Mintimer Shaimiev, was at the time obviously still trying to act as an intermediary to solve the conflict between President Dudayev and the Russian leadership without further bloodshed.

Within a few weeks after the conference, I was notified by

President Shaimiev's office that the Republic of Tatarstan made a decision to close the Tatarstan Plenipotentiary Representative Office in Australia.

Shortly afterwards, the Russian Ambassador in Canberra paid a visit to Adelaide and met with me privately to convey his advice that I should not visit the Russian Federation (and Tatarstan) for five years. He told me that he expected that everything about the conference in Warsaw and the presentation made there would be forgotten after five years and it would be safe for me to travel to Russia for a visit again, if I wanted to do so, as my FSB records would be expunged by then.

Subsequently, in that period, Tatarstan did buy a large cargo plane-load of thoroughbred breeder cattle from Australia to improve livestock quality in Tatarstan by using the intermediary services of a Russian importer, who had bought from me at SAMCOR frozen beef tripe and liver offal to import into Russia and sell to the consumers there as a low-cost protein supplement in addition to beef or mutton.

Years later, the new President of Tatarstan, Rustam Minnikhanov—who replaced President Mintimer Shaimiev—did pay a two-day visit to South Australia on his privately chartered, small jet to be met and greeted by me and the South Australian Government officials, with South Australian Minister, Jack Snelling, hosting a banquet on his behalf. That visit, however, did not result in any tangible business activity between South Australia and Tatarstan in the aftermath of his visit, except perhaps some Australian rice, processed meat products and wine that by coincidence appeared in the supermarkets in Kazan as well as in Moscow.

After I closed the abattoir operation in 1999, I had to wait four years to secure the re-zoning of SAMCOR land from 'Special Abattoir' to 'Commercial Zone' by the South Australian Government. The commercial zone gave me the chance to sell the remaining land parcels and to make reasonable revenue out of the whole SAMCOR enterprise that had dragged on for nearly ten years since 1996. It became obvious that most of the revenue made from the sale would end up in the government coffers by way of the Capital Gains tax and ongoing Land Holding tax, unless I rolled over most of it into similar land development projects. So, I ended up buying a 45-acre land parcel adjacent to Mount Hotham Airport in the year 2000 and building a ski lodge on the land. Once the SAMCOR land sales were settled, I decided to make some residential development land acquisitions in Tasmania, located on the outskirts of Hobart, from 2005 onwards. Thus started another 15-year saga of developing and selling residential allotments in Bridgewater, Granton and New Norfolk, which ended up being initially just a struggle for survival commercially, battling the local council and the state government bureaucracy for endless approval permits and selling land parcels virtually at cost to stay afloat.

Eventually, around 2020, the prices attainable for land and houses increased to the point that allowed me and my extended family, whom I brought into the development project to make some money for them as well, to exit the real estate market in New Norfolk on reasonably profitable terms.

As my ski lodge was located next to Mount Hotham Airport, in 2007 I decided to buy a small twin-engine turbo diesel Diamond DA42 aircraft made in Austria to enjoy flying to the ski lodge from South Australia rather than driving 1,200 kilometres there on country roads. By then I had already undertaken the necessary training and secured a private pilot's licence. I had to go to Austria to take delivery of the brand-new DA42 aircraft from the factory after I paid for it in full early in the year 2007.

At the factory, I was put through a training course on a G-1000 glass cockpit simulator as well as undertaking flight training on an aircraft similar to the one I had purchased over a one-month period with a flying instructor until I was deemed proficient to fly the twin-engine, five-seater DA42 aircraft on my own.

To fly the aircraft from Austria to Australia I had to hire an experienced ferry pilot, who flew it for me until I met him at Alice Springs Airport. I joined him there to fly the aircraft to Adelaide Parafield Airport. I rented a hangar space to store the aircraft when I was not flying it. For the first three years I had an enjoyable time flying to the ski lodge next to Mount Hotham Airport and back to Adelaide, and flying to Queensland and NSW with my family members and friends, finding travel by air far more comfortable than driving long distances by car.

One day in May of 2010, I made the mistake of taking off from Mount Hotham Airport ignoring a strong westerly wind forecast. So, a flight that would normally take two-and-a-half hours to reach Adelaide from Mount Hotham took me nearly four hours in strong headwinds. By the time I reached Murray Bridge near Adelaide, cloud cover over Adelaide Hills descended to below 1,000 metres. As I was already running low on fuel due to strong headwinds, I decided just to land the aircraft at Parafield Airport rather than diverting it to Goolwa or some other unfamiliar airstrip. I was fully instrument-trained in Austria to fly the aircraft in foggy conditions, so it did not occur to me that I did not have an instrument rating endorsed on my Australian private pilot's licence. I did land the aircraft in cloud conditions slightly below 1,000 metres at Parafield Airport without any difficulty or causing any distress to anybody at Parafield.

Somehow, somebody at Parafield Airport must have reported the arrival of my aircraft on that day in foggy conditions as I received a phone call from the Civil Aviation Safety Authority office in Adelaide the next day telling me to report to their office.

Without worrying much about it, I did report to the Civil Aviation Safety Authority (CASA) office only to be told that my private pilot's licence would be suspended. My argument that I had undergone instrument flight training in Austria did not go well with CASA, despite providing them with a written statement to that effect from the Diamond Aircraft Factory in Austria. They simply rejected it by saying that I should have had an instrument flight rating endorsed on my private pilot's licence in Australia.

I ended up hiring aviation lawyers to dispute my case through the Arbitration Commission. I continued flying my aircraft while the matter dragged on for another three years, costing me a fair amount in legal fees. In the end, I decided to give up and just sell the aircraft to the highest bidder. Thus ended my saga with CASA in 2014, despite the fact that I did not endanger my or anybody else's life by crashing the aircraft from getting disorientated in foggy conditions as feared by CASA. I often flew the aircraft into or out of Mount Hotham Airport, which has an elevation of 1,300 metres above sea level and a small water reservoir next to it and was deemed to be the highest-altitude airport in Australia. CASA officials obviously did not like my name and decided to cancel my private pilot's licence regardless of the circumstances of the case or giving consideration to my flying ability, or to the fact that I had clocked up more than 500 flying hours by then without endangering anybody's lives.

I ended up selling my DA42 aircraft in 2015 at a small loss and concentrated my efforts on land development projects in Tasmania in the outer suburb of Hobart called New Norfolk, adding a brand new area with more than 200 houses, and the local Derwent Valley Council naming two of the streets in the area—Sadri Court and Leila Street—after my surname and my mother's name.

This became our substantial contribution to the endemic housing shortages in the Hobart area in Tasmania in the last fifteen years. This valuable contribution to the Tasmanian low-cost housing market was in addition to the major shopping centre development on the former SAMCOR land in the Adelaide suburb of Gepps Cross in South Australia, which became the largest shopping centre as well as a warehouse storage facility in South Australia.

Since coming to Australia in February 1976 as refugees from China, we did well in Australia by not only getting ourselves university educated, but also working hard and, as a result, becoming wealthy, well above general population standards in Australia.

As a former refugee family who struggled to come to Australia out of Communist China for nearly twenty years, we ended up also being instrumental in creating Tatar, Uzbek and Uighur communities of substance in most major cities in Australia.

8

Origins of the Tatar Nation

It is a well-known historical fact that the Tatar nation, which suffered from major military defeat followed by genocide at the hands of their historical Russian enemy, ended up getting their history written by the victorious Russians, who invariably glorified their own hard-won victory and maligned the defeated Tatars as not worthy of any compassion or recognition of their role in history; hence, the long-perpetuated myth of the 'Tatar-Mongol Yoke'.

In reality, the Tatars were not only instrumental to the historical rise of the Russian Empire, but were also forced after their defeat to contribute their best daughters and sons to the advent of the Russian nation through forcible conversion into the Russian Orthodox Church followed by full assimilation over the centuries after the defeat of Khanate of Kazan in October 1552. This fact is colourfully expressed by the Russian proverb: "Scratch a Russian and you shall find a Tatar."

It is a historical fact that the Tatar nation as we know it today, or the Khanate of Bulgar, as it was known prior to the Mongol invasion and their conquest of Eurasia in 1220s, was prosperous. Tatar lands were famous then for steel weaponry, leather and linen goods, with established trading links on the so-called 'Silk Road', and included the Khanate of Bulgar. The Tatar nation not only first bore the brunt of the Mongol army's military might under Chenghiz Khan, but subsequently became known as the 'Tatars', often leading the avant-garde Mongol forces due to their outstanding bravery on the battlefield.

Chenghiz Khan's generals were so impressed with the Tatars' bravery—who even initially succeeded in inflicting a military defeat on the avant-garde Mongol invaders—that they decided to invite the Tatar forces, after their eventual defeat and the destruction of their capital city of Bulgar, to join the Mongol army on honourable terms rather than decimating them altogether. Subsequently, the Tatar forces led the avant-garde Mongol army to conquer the disunited Russian principalities (kniazhestva) with minimal losses to the Mongol core by the invading army.

Having conquered, pacified and united all the Russian principalities from 1223 onwards, Batu Khan, the grandson of Chenghiz Khan, incorporated them all into the Empire of Golden Horde, otherwise then known also as 'Ulus Jochi', named after the father of Batu and the eldest son of Chenghiz Khan.

It was the Golden Horde which ruled Russian principalities

for well over 250 years with a firm hand, levying taxes as well as protecting them from their external enemies from the west, protecting them also from indulging in internal strife endemic to the Russian kniazhestva in the past prior to being subjugated by the Tatars.

Yassa, or the law of the Mongol Empire, established under Chenghiz Khan after his conquests of Eurasia, was accomplished by creating the biggest empire of all time, stretching from Asia-Pacific to Central Europe, and was very progressive and much ahead of its time, being applied equally to all the subjects of his vast Empire, without any exemptions to the ruling Mongols or the non-Mongol vassals subject to the Mongol rule.

Chenghiz Khan also established efficient horse relay communication and courier transportation systems, which stretched from one end of his vast empire to the other, encompassing most of the Eurasian Continent. Yassa and the communication systems established then were not only progressive and well ahead of their time, but were also very practical in controlling and ruling the Mongol-Tatar Empire efficiently, leading to economic development and prosperity of the vast empire that encompassed many nations, with Turkic, or in other words, the early Tatar language as the lingua franca of many Turkic dialects as well as the ruling minority Mongol language.

Exceptional cruelty to his enemies in wartime, often attributed to Chenghiz Khan, did take place during his conquests. In most cases, however, it was applied to punish those Mongol as well as Turkic tribes who hurt him and his extended clan badly during his younger years, when he was known as young Lord Temuchin, having lost his father and tribal assets to the treachery of neighbouring tribes.

Originally, his attractive mother was kidnapped and married by his father from the neighbouring Merkit tribe, who was obviously not Mongol but Turkic-speaking; hence, the blond hair and non-Mongol appearance often attributed to Chenghiz Khan. The Merkit tribesmen sealed their fate, eventually annihilated after many years, and later kidnapping young Temuchin's beloved wife as a retaliatory gesture against his late father. This was done to punish him as a payback to his long-dead father, even after he had been treacherously killed by his enemies by being offered poisoned koumiss, or fermented mare's milk, which Temuchin's father had to accept as a symbolic return gesture expressing friendship.

Other cases of the exceptional cruelty of Mongols took place when Chenghiz Khan's high-ranking emissaries, sent to negotiate and offer surrender terms to avoid bloodshed, were murdered as a response to the offer of surrender. Such a treacherous act would seal the fate of the brainless ruler and the settlement in question for total annihilation and destruction, as the lives of the high-ranking Mongol envoys sent to negotiate were regarded as sacrosanct to both sides and subject to total immunity under Chenghiz Khan's Yassa law. Those adversaries who treated Mongol emissaries with respect and fairness and negotiated with them were spared such a fate, often ending up surrendering peacefully in order to become a part of the Mongol Empire under Chenghiz Khan.

The Russian 'Kniaz'ya', or native Russian overlords, ended up competing among themselves after their defeat by Batu Khan's forces to become the faithful vassals of the Golden Horde by visiting the capital city of Sarai and eagerly drinking koumiss to prove their allegiance to their Tatar rulers on ceremonial occasions. These same Russians, as the faithful subjects of the Golden Horde Empire, were gradually taught not only to fight bravely when waging wars against common external enemies, but even how to ride on horseback properly, wearing trousers instead of traditional Russian long gowns, or kaftans.

One such event is colourfully described in the Russian chronicles as the battle of Chudskoe Ozero (Chudskoe Lake), whereby the heavy armour-clad cavalry of the invading Teutonic Order was defeated by the Tatar light cavalry skilfully using ropes and pulling them off their horses down onto the ice of the Chudskoe Lake where the heavy armour-clad enemy knights could not even get onto their feet because of the slippery ice. Naturally, the Russian chronicles attributed the victory to Kniaz Alexander Nevsky, who in fact was part of the Russian force subservient to the Tatars and under their command during the battle, as they peacefully surrendered to the Tatar-Mongol rule in 1238 and became part of the Mongol Empire. The Tatar light horse cavalry, which attacked the heavy armour-clad Teutonic knights' cavalry on the ice of the lake, played a decisive role in inflicting total defeat on the invading knights of the Teutonic Order.

It is a historical fact that Golden Horde Tatars did not just extract tribute from their Russian vassals, but also protected them from previous endemic internal strife as well as external enemy intrusions into the Russian-inhabited lands. Their Russian vassals were not only allowed to practice their Orthodox Christianity in peace, but also encouraged to contribute to the prosperity of the Russian Orthodox Church and its assets, thus leading to the golden age of Orthodox Russian Christianity, which happened to coincide with the Tatar rule, whilst the Russian Tsars later in history often plundered the Church coffers to finance their wars of conquest, sometimes even melting church bells into cannons.

It should also be pointed out that while most of Europe as well as Russia were backward and messy in every meaning of the word, the cities of the Golden Horde, such as the capital city of Sarai, already had plumbing and central heating in its palaces, and well-designed and constructed paved streets, as described with astonishment by the foreign visitors to Sarai at the time.

As is often the case in history, the Mongol-Tatar Empire disintegrated into smaller khanates as a result of the splitting up of the dynastic rulers of the fourth and fifth generations. Thus, the Golden Horde's fortunes also declined when Tamerlane invaded these lands at the end of the fourteenth century. Tamerlane, who was inflicted with lameness during his early years as a horse thief and a ruthless robber, was spared death by a compassionate merchant whose caravan Tamerlane had unsuccessfully attacked earlier to plunder. The merchant then made the big mistake of not killing him when the defeated and maimed robber begged for his life. This merchant's mistake, driven by compassion, was to change the course of fourteenth-century history when Tamerlane assembled a large cohort of ruthless robbers like himself and led them to kill hundreds of thousands of Turkic-speaking people of the time.

Tamerlane eventually became the builder and cruel ruler of his vast marauding empire, not only destroying the Ottoman Turkish Sultan, Bayezid, and confining him to a cage, but also eventually attacking the Empire of Golden Horde to the north as well. Tamerlane did not succeed in completely defeating Khan Tokhtamysh of the Golden Horde in 1398, who a few years earlier had been depending on him as a subservient ally, but nonetheless destroyed Khan Tokhtamysh's military might without conquering and thus weakening the Russian principalities further to the north due to the onset of the cold winter.

Tamerlane changed the course of the fifteenth century because as a result of his onslaught, the Golden Horde ended up eventually disintegrating into four separate khanates of Crimea, Astrakhan, Kazan and Siberia during the fifteenth century, whereas the Russian principalities that did not experience Tamerlane's onslaught emerged as the unified and independent Russian Kingdom of Muscovy. Tatars themselves were instrumental in the creation of the unified Russian Tsardom of Muscovy, as they entrusted the Muscovite ruler, Ivan Kalita (Ivan Halta the Bagger), to collect tribute, or taxes for the Alte, from all of the Russian-speaking principalities. Ivan Kalita embezzled enough wealth as well as power for himself in the process, thus becoming the first Russian Tsar in his own right.

In this context it should be emphasised once again that historically the Tatar rulers not only tolerated the Russian Orthodox Church, but also strengthened it by exempting it from taxes. Over more than two-and-a-half centuries of the so-called 'Tatar Yoke' myth, the unified Russian Tsardom subservient to Tatar rule as well as the Russian Orthodox Church prospered in reality, experiencing the period of Orthodox Christian religious renaissance all over Tatar-ruled Russia. The Russian peasantry also enjoyed freedoms under Tatar rule as free subjects of the Golden Horde under the

Yassa codex as long as they paid their taxes and levies. They ended up eventually getting enslaved by their Russian rulers into a serfdom system, once the Russian rulers became fully independent and ended up conquering the Tatar Khanates, establishing the unified Russian empire in the process.

It was the Russian Orthodox Church—led then by the ruthless priests, Sylvester and Protopop (Bishop) Makariy—who not only succeeded in installing cowardly and cruel Ivan the Terrible as the ruler of the unified Russian Kingdom in the 1540s, but also planned and orchestrated the conquest and total destruction of the Khanate of Kazan in October 1552, decimating its population in the process.

This conquest accomplished almost total annihilation of the inhabitants of the besieged city and surrounds of Kazan, whereby more than 82,000 of them were slaughtered and thrown into the Volga River to frighten inhabitants of the Khanate of Astrakhan downstream into unconditional surrender. It also forced the survivors of the Khanate of Kazan, who did not manage to escape the mass slaughter, to forcibly convert to Orthodox Christianity, or be killed and thrown into the Volga River as a punishment for the refusal to convert.

This systematic forcible conversion into the Russian Orthodox Church continued for centuries from 1552, offering both severe floggings as punishment for refusal to convert, and inducements to become prominent members of the Russian Orthodox Society by joining the ruling elite, when converting. This policy was advanced especially efficiently during the three centuries of reign of the Romanov dynasty, when a large proportion of the Russian nobility—the best and the brightest—were Tatars converted to serve the Russian Empire, starting with Tsar Boris (Saburov) Godunov, who was also a Tatar converted to the Orthodox faith in order to make him the Tsar of Russia by the Orthodox Church. Boris Godunov ruled Russia with a firm hand for seven years from 1598–1605, strengthening the power of the Orthodox Church in the process. When he suddenly died in somewhat mysterious circumstances in 1605, his unexplained death triggered the 'Time of Troubles' (Smutnoe Vremya).

Many famous names of the Russian nobility—statesmen as well as military elite such as Minin, who saved Russia from being conquered by the Polish invaders, General Kutuzov who saved Russia from the French invaders by defeating Napoleon, General Suvorov, Admiral Nakhimov, Count Sheremetev, who owned more than 200,000 serfs, prominent writers and intellectuals such as Turgenev, Chaadayev, Bulgakov, Bunin and so on—were, in fact, Russians with Tatar ancestry who assimilated into the Russian elite, among many others too numerous to list here.

The so-called 'Tatar Yoke' often referred to in official Russian and Soviet publications was nothing but a myth first invented by the Russian Orthodox priests to justify their mistreatment and forcible conversion of Tatars into the Russian Orthodox Church in order to fully assimilate them as well as to enslave them into serfdom. In fact, the creation of the institution of serfdom, or enslavement of close to 20 million peasants of central and southern Russia, coincided with the advent of the Romanov Dynasty in Russia. Peasants, who were free subjects of the Tatar Empire of Golden Horde during the two-and-a-half centuries of Tatar rule under Yassa, became a tradeable commodity under the Russian tsars, who could be sold and bought by their masters at whim, together with the land on which they toiled for their livelihood, to earn revenue for their masters. Only the emancipation edict of 1861 decreed during the reign of Emperor Alexander the Second abolished serfdom, or enslavement of the Russian peasantry, which lasted for well over two centuries.

The atheistic Russian communist state, which came to power after the October 1917 revolution, subsequently not only adopted the myth of the 'Tatar Yoke' to justify similar Russian assimilation policies targeting the Tatars alongside other non-Russian ethnic minorities, but also re-introduced the twentieth-century equivalent form of the Soviet state-imposed serfdom of the entire Soviet peasant class under the disguise of so-called 'collective farms' or 'kolkhozy', established in 1932 under the murderous Stalinist regime. Inhabitants of the kolkhozy were prohibited from leaving their registered places of abode similar to the serfs who belonged to their landlord 'masters', the only difference then being that Stalin's Soviet state became their new master, controlling their places of work as well as their movements outside of their settlements or places of residence.

This wanton exploitation of Soviet peasantry as the twentieth-century Soviet state-owned serfs enabled Stalin to forcibly effect rapid industrialisation of the Soviet Union in the 1930s by plundering the peasantry of their produce and even exporting it abroad while starving the entire peasant population of the Soviet Union. Starvation and death from hunger among the peasants of Ukraine and other parts of the Soviet Union post-WW2, after 1945, is a well-documented fact.

After the disintegration of the Soviet Union in 1991, close to 10 million Tatars remain as part and parcel of the disintegrated modern-day Russian Empire, faithfully serving in all walks of life and contributing their talents to the advancement of Russian State interests. Close to 5 million Tatars live in the so-called 'autonomous' Republics of Tatarstan and Bashkortostan in the European part of Russia to the west of the Ural Mountains range which separates Europe from Asia.

There are also large Tatar communities in most major Russian cities such as Moscow, St Petersburg, Samara, Astrakhan, and so on, who have successfully blended in with the Russians and prefer not to reveal their Tatar ethnicity, unless talking to another Tatar in their own language.

Yet, the demise of the Kazan Khanate at the hands of Ivan the Terrible and Protopop Makariy was a historical aberration that could have been easily avoided if the Empire of Golden Horde did not end up disintegrating into the four separate khanates of Kazan, Astrakhan, Crimea and Siberia.

This disintegration of the Golden Horde into four separate khanates was the direct result of the war waged by Tamerlane against Khan Tokhtamysh of the Golden Horde, which also caused protracted internal strife with the Eastern Mongol rulers of the time.

These four Tatar khanates were also weakened further by the advent of the Bubonic Plague which originated from central China in the mid-fourteenth century, killing a significant proportion of their populations on the way after spreading through the so-called 'Silk Road' interacting with the European kingdoms. The Russian principalities to the north were spared such a fate at the time due to their remoteness as well as the colder climatic conditions that prevented the influx of rats, which spread out of central China carrying the plague with them along the 'Silk Road'.

The migrating rats decimated populations throughout most

of Eurasia, spreading into Tatar-inhabited lands in 1445–1448 as well, which at the time already enjoyed close trading and communication links with the rest of Europe, being prominently located on the 'Silk Road'.

It should also be pointed out that the city of St Petersburg was built on orders from Peter 'the Great' by forcibly bringing in and utilising mostly hard-working Tatar tradesmen, builders and architects after forcibly bringing them in from their native lands in the Volga-Ural region and working them to death to clear swampy land on the banks of the Neva River and to build a modern, European-style city with colourful architectural features influenced by Tatar architects, to turn it into the capital of the Russian Empire. More than 100,000 Tatar workers perished over the decades of forced hard work in the process of fulfilling the dream of Emperor Peter 'the Great'.

These facts summarise seven centuries of Tatar-Russian interaction and point out the Golden Horde foundations of the modern Russian Empire.

9

Tatars in Australia and the World

Tatars in Australia belong to one of its smallest and least-known ethnic groups. The first Tatars to step onto Australian soil were a few railway workers who came with their Russian compatriots during the railway boom years at the end of the nineteenth century. Most of them returned to their homeland or ended up getting assimilated into the Australian community. After WW2, some Tatars came from German labour camps or displaced persons' camps as well as from Latvia and Poland, in the aftermath of the war. Most of the more recent Tatar settlers in Adelaide came from East Turkestan, or in other words, from Xinjiang of China, from 1976 onwards, helped by the Australian Government under the 'White Russian' refugee intake and resettlement program. The Sadri family—who succeeded in getting exit visas from the Chinese authorities after nineteen years of struggle to migrate to Australia rather than getting repatriated to the Soviet Union—were the first to arrive on 11 February 1976. They then made a concerted effort to help the remaining members of their small Tatar community in Xinjiang to secure visas to come to Australia as well, spending a lot of their time and their hard-earned money to secure sponsorships and relocation expenses during the following ten years after their arrival in Australia. There are now approximately 500 Australians of Tatar background, living predominantly in Adelaide, Sydney and Melbourne, with a few more in Brisbane, Canberra and Hobart.

In their homeland and in the former Soviet Union, Tatars now number close to 12 million people, making them the largest ethnic minority in Russia overall. In terms of their religious orientation, the majority of Tatars count themselves as Muslims of Sunni background, although a small percentage adhere to Orthodox Christianity after getting forcibly converted since the fall of the Kingdom of Kazan in October 1552.

There are large professional groups of Tatars in major capital cities of the Russian Federation, and the Republic of Tatarstan in the Volga basin is one of the most industrialised regions in the country with a concentration of a number of strategically important manufacturing industries, such as aircraft and truck building facilities. Over 2 million Tatars live in the adjoining Republic of Bashkortostan, or Bashkiria, where they outnumber the Bashkirs and comprise the majority of the population of the Republic. This territorial anomaly was deliberately created by the Soviet leadership to reduce the size as well as Tatar population numbers in adjoining Tatarstan.

Over half a million Crimean Tatars, on the other hand, are still struggling to return and establish themselves in their former homes on the Crimean Peninsula after being deported on Stalin's orders to Siberia and Central Asia at the end of WW2. Some 46 per cent of their numbers at the time are believed to have perished by starvation and diseases deliberately inflicted on them in exile in the years following their ethnic cleansing from the Crimean Peninsula through forced mass deportation.

Outside of the former Soviet Union, Tatar communities now live in Finland, Poland, Romania, America and Turkey. A few families also live in China, Japan, Germany, the Czech Republic and Canada. The members of the Tatar Association of South Australia do their best to maintain informal contacts as well as internet links, not only with their compatriots in Tatarstan and the republics of the former Soviet Union, but also with the Tatar communities in the abovementioned countries. There are a number of internet websites where further information on Tatars and Tatarstan can be obtained. As mentioned earlier, the majority of Tatars came to Australia with their families from China and the former Soviet Union over the last four-and-a-half decades, although the earliest Tatar settlers comprised mostly refugees, including those who came via Turkey, Japan and Korea in the aftermath of WW2.

In 1978, whilst studying at the University of Adelaide, Roostam Sadri prepared the Constitution of the Tatar

Association of South Australia, which was formally inaugurated early in 1980 as an incorporated body.

Mrs Lailya Sadri was then elected as the first Honorary President of the Tatar Association of South Australia and gave, together with her husband, Mr Sagit Sadri, her son, Roostam, and daughter, Nailya, many years of tireless, dedicated service to the fledgling Tatar community, often spending their hard-earned family money and time to help others to settle into their new lives in Australia. From 1978 until the late 1990s, the Tatar Association of South Australia under their leadership not only provided orientation and assistance for newly arrived migrants, such as initial accommodation, furniture and food, as well as help with finding employment, but most importantly exerted considerable effort in obtaining sponsorships or actually sponsoring remaining members of the Tatar community in Xinjiang, who were still enduring political and racial persecution from the Chinese communist authorities.

Early in 1977, Roostam Sadri qualified as a contract interpreter and translator for the Russian language with the Department of Immigration in Adelaide. At the same time, he enrolled at the University of Adelaide to study for the Bachelor of Arts degree, majoring in International Relations, History, Economics and Linguistics. As a member of the Adelaide University Liberal Club, he met with former Senator Baden Teague. Roostam Sadri wrote:

My friends at the Liberal Club, having learned of the plight of the Tatar prisoners in Communist China, arranged a meeting for me with the then Minister for Foreign Affairs, the Honourable Andrew Peacock, to whom I presented a petition. This petition asked for his help in securing the release of the ethnic Tatar prisoners in China—Nael Gabitov and Tashmuhammed Umarov—who were distantly related to my family, so that they could come to Australia to join their relatives and friends living here. Subsequently, I learned that both Senator Baden Teague, a member of the Senate Committee on Foreign Affairs and Defence, and Minister Andrew Peacock, took a personal interest in the fate of those prisoners named in the petition, and approached the Chinese authorities with the request to have them released and allowed to migrate to Australia. The Honourable Andrew Peacock MP even requested the Chinese authorities to allow him to travel to Urumchi, the capital city of Xinjiang, and did travel there. Paradoxically, it was this compassionate appeal to the Chinese authorities by the Australian Minister, Andrew Peacock, as well as Senator Baden Teague, that embarrassed the Chinese Foreign Affairs officials to release the Soviet ex-consular workers, who had been detained in China without trial for almost 19 years, where two of the detainees even died in prison, as the Soviet diplomats in Beijing did not even lift a finger to secure the release of their former employees and

Soviet citizens. In 1986, Roostam Sadri accompanied Senator Baden Teague to China as his interpreter, visiting Shanghai, Beijing, Urumchi and Kuldja (Yining) with him and members of his entourage. At that time, most of the aforementioned families had already been released from prison and issued visas to migrate to Australia.

In 1980, Mrs Lailya Sadri organised a small group of Tatar youth to perform Tatar dances accompanied by Tatar music at the Adelaide University Theatre Hall, to introduce Tatar culture to this country. She designed and personally sewed all of the Tatar national costumes for the occasion.

In 1984, Mr Azrail Abid (Gabitov) organised and opened the Tatar Language Ethnic School, with assistance from the Ethnic Schools Association of South Australia, to teach the Tatar children their native tongue on weekends. These Tatar language courses have been functioning ever since, teaching the Tatar language and the basics of their religion to the children of the Tatar community in Adelaide. Many years later, these duties were taken over by Imam Bulat Ishmuhammed, who had been sent from Tatarstan to also teach the Tatar children their native language at the Lailya Sadri Tatar Community Centre in Adelaide, which was formally opened for the purpose early in 2013.

In 1986, Mrs Lailya Sadri organised for the Tatar community to participate in a festival commemorating the 150th anniversary of European settlement in South

Australia. During that festival a small group of former professional Tatar artists performed Tatar songs and folk dances on stage to great applause from the public present. Tatar national dishes and snacks were also offered to the public from a food stall run by the Tatar Association and proved very popular with the general public. The Tatar Association from its inception not only provided initial orientation for newly arrived migrants and assistance with accommodation and employment, but most importantly exerted considerable effort in sponsoring the remaining members of their Sinkiang community still enduring political and racial persecution from the Chinese authorities who had embarked on a campaign of ethnic cleansing.

Despite great difficulties encountered in procuring entry visas for them, the Association managed to bring out a substantial number of Tatar as well as Uighur and Uzbek families. These Uighur and Uzbek families in Australia grew in number by sponsoring their relatives and friends, who were also enduring political and racial hardship under the Chinese rule in Sinkiang (Xinjiang), and who gradually became large enough to form their own communities, now living happily and prosperously in Adelaide, Sydney and Melbourne. The Australian Tatar community has done remarkably well in adapting and integrating into their new social and cultural environment in Australia. Most of them speak fluent English in addition to one or two other languages and even those of them who arrived relatively recently make a concerted effort to learn good English to avoid communication difficulties at work.

Most Tatars in Australia own their own homes and are successful in establishing themselves in their new homeland. For instance, Roostam Sadri, with a loan from the State Bank in 1996, purchased from the State Government of South Australia and operated successfully the largest export meat processing plant in South Australia in the late 1990s, known as SAMCOR, which provided, jointly with T & R Pastoral, employment opportunities to more than 600 workers. SAMCOR, which employed quite a few Tatar, Uighur and Uzbek workers at the time to produce Halal meat for export to the Middle East, contributed millions of dollars to the Australian economy by way of Federal, State, and Local Government taxes and levies.

After the closure of SAMCOR in 2000, Roostam Sadri became instrumental in successfully developing the 55-hectare SAMCOR site, located in the middle of Greater Metropolitan Adelaide, 10 km north of the Central Business District, into the biggest shopping and warehousing centre in South Australia. The closure of SAMCOR was due to the government imposition of a five-year deadline on the operation of the abattoir at the site for environmental reasons, and also because T & R Pastoral acquired their own abattoir in Murray Bridge with a financial grant from the State Government of South Australia and therefore stopped working with SAMCOR.

From 1995–2000 Roostam Sadri also represented the

Republic of Tatarstan in Australia and in 1996 organised a visit of the Tatarstan Government Delegation to South Australia. The 82-member delegation was headed by the then Prime Minister, the Honourable Farid Mukhametshin, and was hosted by the South Australian Government led by the Honourable Premier, Dean Brown. The Tatar community overall thrived in the free political and economic environment in Australia, and a few young members of the community graduated from Australian universities to become practising doctors, lawyers and builders, in addition to a few successful business owners and company directors doing business in most state capital cities. Sagit Sadri, together with his wife, Lailya Sadri, and their youngest son, Ramil Sadri, went to Tatarstan in 1989 to commemorate the approaching 1,100th anniversary of the adoption of Islam by the Volga Tatars of the Kingdom of Bulgar in the year 922 AD. Subsequently, both Sagit Sadri and Lailya Sadri participated in the World Tatar Congress in Kazan, Tatarstan, in 1992 and gave presentations there.

Lailya Sadri, like her mother, Aysha Gabitov, was an accomplished poet as well as a writer. Her poems in Tatar titled *Haerle Duga* as well as her book, *Ghumur Yule,* were published in Kazan in both 2000 and 2003. Sagit Sadri also published his memoirs in a book, *Tatar Bashe Niyne Kurmy.*

Nailya worked as an Interpreter and Bilingual Information Officer for the Department of Immigration and Ethnic Affairs and as a Bilingual Community Consultant with the

Department of Prime Minister and Cabinet. She also worked concurrently as a volunteer teacher at the Tatar Ethnic School. Nailya, together with her husband and the Sadri family, assisted Tatar, Uzbek and Uighur migrants with their settlement needs, never turning away anybody who came to them seeking help.

On 29 September 2011, His Excellency Mr Rustam Minnikhanov, President of the Republic of Tatarstan, awarded both Sagit Sadri and Lailya Sadri Certificates of Appreciation for their many years of dedicated service to the Tatar community in Australia. Similarly, Roostam Sadri and Nailya also received Award Certificates for their community service.

In 2009, Sagit and Lailya Sadri celebrated their 70th Wedding Anniversary with the Tatar community in Adelaide. Lailya Sadri passed away in Adelaide on 8 August 2012. In March 2013, her son, Roostam Sadri, together with all other members of the extended Sadri family, opened the Lailya Sadri Community Centre in Adelaide, dedicated to her memory, with the premises available for Tatar language classes as well as a prayer room and venue for community functions.

On 19 August 2017, Sagit Sadri received congratulatory letters from Her Majesty Queen Elizabeth II, His Excellency General the Honourable Sir Peter Cosgrove AK MC, Governor-General of the Commonwealth of Australia, and his wife, Lynne, and the Honourable Malcolm Turnbull MP,

Prime Minister of Australia, honouring the 100th anniversary of his birthday. Sagit Sadri passed away on 1 January 2018.

10

Totalitarian Rule of Xi Jinping in Modern China

In recent years, Communist China has emerged as a major military and political force, rivalling the United States in the international arena. It is no coincidence that this has overlapped with Chairman Xi Jinping's unprecedented implementation of policies of wanton internal oppression of the entire population of China, resulting in unbridled genocide of the ethnic minorities, especially Muslim ethnic minorities of East Turkestan[1], the Buddhist ethnic minority of Tibet as well as millions of Chinese followers of Falun Gong.[2] The communist regime perceived the Falun Gong followers as a real threat to the unrestrained rule of the Communist Party, deciding to eradicate the teachings of Falun Gong in China altogether. The murderous Xi Jinping regime resorted to the unprecedented practice of detaining millions of Falun Gong followers as well as Muslim ethnic minorities in concentration camps.

1 Or as the Chinese call it now: The New Frontier "Xinjiang Uighur Autonomous Region of China"

2 Also known as Falun Da Fa — a spiritual practice of meditative exercises and moral teachings propagating truthfulness, compassion and tolerance

The ethnic minorities especially, suffered total deprivation of their basic human rights, being forced *en masse* either to assimilate fully into the Han Chinese culture and to speak only Chinese as their first language, or to gradually perish in the so-called 're-education labour' concentration camps built to gradually exterminate the detainees through starvation and hard labour. The newly rich or prominent Chinese regarded disloyal by the Xi Jinping clique and therefore a threat to his unbridled rule through his Communist Party apparatus, have also not escaped the latest purges, many of them disappearing into the so-called 're-education labour camps', or even getting executed. Any wealthy or prominent person in China not affiliated with the ruling communist Xi regime can now be accused of tax evasion, disloyalty to the Xi Jinping clique, or being a hidden adherent of Falun Gong with relative ease, if deemed necessary.

These repressive policies resort even to intrusive video surveillance of each and every family formed into units of 20–200 families, each unit headed by one security official who is obligated to report to the security services on a regular basis. It is therefore not a surprise that these oppressive measures resulted in a fivefold increase in asylum seeker numbers out of China in 2019 alone, especially into bordering Central Asian republics to the north, prior to the lockdown of borders as a result of the ongoing COVID-19 pandemic. More than 2 million Muslim ethnic minority detainees, predominantly including Uighurs, Kazakhs, Kyrgyz and Uzbeks, are being starved to death from mass imprisonment and torture in concentration camps during vicious interrogations.

Numerous cases of suicides or murder-suicides have, as a manifestation of desperate resistance, become widespread in ethnic minority areas of Xinjiang (East Turkestan) as well as in Tibet or Chinese-controlled inner Mongolia.

So-called 'strike hard' policies being announced and implemented by the Xi Jinping clique since his advent to power in 2012, especially singled out close to 12 million Muslim Uighurs of Xinjiang as well as the Buddhist Tibetans of Tibet and the surrounding regions, who constitute the two largest surviving ethnic minorities inhabiting East Turkestan (Xinjiang) and Tibet.

The Muslim population of Xinjiang, or (New Frontier) Uighur 'Autonomous' Region, with a currently estimated non-Han Chinese population of around 14 million people, comprises close to 12 million Uighurs, but also approximately 2 million Kazakhs, Mongols, Kyrgyz, Tajiks, Uzbeks and Salars as well as a very small number of Turkmen, Afghans and Tatars. They have been hit by these oppressive policies especially hard, with more than 2 million of them being detained in these extermination camps, effectively leaving no ethnic minority family untouched by these brutally repressive policies. In most cases, both husband and wife of the same family are incarcerated, with children left either to starve to death or be dispatched into government-run orphanages where they are allowed only to speak Han Chinese as their first language of communication and have only Han Chinese names. The young Muslim women, once imprisoned, are routinely raped and tortured by their Chinese interrogators, often getting sterilised in the process.

Chen Quanguo, the current Communist Party henchman of Chairman Xi Jinping in Xinjiang, after imprisoning and slaughtering large numbers of Tibetans in Tibet, especially the Tibetan monks, was promoted by Chairman Xi to lead a similar slaughter of the Muslim population of Xinjiang as well. As a de facto commander of the security forces in Xinjiang, he was instrumental in the rapid build-up and expansion of a vast network of massive detention facilities as well as forced labour camps, all done by the forced labour of the detainees themselves.

It is reliably estimated that well over 2 million people—mostly adult Uighurs, as well as members of all other abovementioned groups—are being detained in the vast network of so-called 're-education' camps, where torture, starvation and brainwashing through repeated application of pro-Chinese and pro-Chairman Xi slogans to be memorised and repeatedly uttered aloud and chanted by the inmates, is practised on a massive scale. The latest satellite imagery available clearly depicts and confirms this estimate in addition to the collection of biometric data and surveillance equipment installed to monitor the movements of the entire Muslim population, which is routinely compiled and stored by the Chairman Xi regime. Eyewitness accounts of visitors to the area also reveal the shocking extent of repression applied to the native non-Han Muslim population of Xinjiang.

Even more shockingly, many among those abovementioned groups who are young enough, well-educated and deemed to be non-receptive to the Chinese Communist Party's 're-education' efforts, disappear and are dispatched to be utilised for organ harvesting to treat and restore the health of Chairman Xi's henchmen and the Communist Chinese elite, as well as for a limited number of well-paying foreigners who used to go to China for treatment prior to the COVID-19 pandemic.

Chairman Xi is not the first Chinese dictator to implement such policies of wanton oppression of the non-Han Chinese population, especially of the ethnic minorities of East Turkestan (Xinjiang), who constitute less than one per cent of the overall population of China.

Non-Han ethnic minorities in China used to inhabit more than half of its present-day territory, especially if Manchuria

(Dongbei) is included. Many millions of Manchurians have been successfully and fully assimilated by the Han Chinese under the Chinese communist regime (with less than fifty individuals overall now still able to speak the Manchu language), whereas the Uighurs, the Tibetans, the Mongols, the Kazakhs and several other ethnic minority groups are still struggling to retain their distinct languages and have managed to survive to a large extent Mao's 'Great Leap Forward' as well as his 'labour re-education' concentration camps and the so-called 'Cultural Revolution', manifested by Nazi-style burning of 'Yellow' books and by parading tied-up intellectuals in the streets in order to humiliate them before sending them to 'labour re-education' death camps.

Chairman Mao and his henchmen did not have the sophisticated hi-tech surveillance and monitoring equipment as well as funding that is now available to Chairman Xi's murderous regime.

Ever since the death of Deng Xiaoping in 1987, a periodic clampdown on the rights and freedoms of ethnic minorities in China, as well as Chinese followers of Falun Gong, has been applied in a wave-like fashion, especially escalating throughout China's ethnic minority-inhabited regions from the 1990s onwards.

Prior to communist rule, Chinese control over East Turkestan, starting with the re-conquest of the region by General Tzo Tzung Tang of the Qing Dynasty of 1882–84, was sporadic and often temporary in nature between periods of full independence or self-rule, often under nominal adherence to the central government of China.

The more recent selective economic prosperity of China was brought about by the quasi-free market reforms implemented during the Deng Xiaoping era, who declared when beginning his reforms in 1978 that, 'it does not matter if the cat is white or black, as long as it is able to catch mice'. This ended Chairman Mao's obsession after his death in 1976, the endemic persecution of educated, hardworking, middle-class Chinese citizens by the indiscriminate application of his concept of 'class struggle'.

Chinese internal economic reforms, which gathered a rapid pace from 1978 onwards under the leadership of Deng Xiaoping, freed up incentives for the influential members of the Communist Party to strive for success through combined embezzlement of state assets as well as hard work. This was enhanced by the import tax-free economic support of China by the American leadership, started by President Nixon and continuing unabated until the Trump era. This gradually led to improved living conditions in China overall as well as the unprecedented increase of Chinese financial and military might globally. These policies conceived by the American leadership of the time to counter the perceived threat from the Soviet Union, appear now to have backfired on the Americans by making the murderous Chairman Xi's regime the dominant threat to American economic interests as well as military might globally.

This environment emboldened Chairman Xi Jinping, after his ascent to supreme power in China in 2012, to adopt domineering and increasingly aggressive policies towards China's neighbours, except Russia. Chairman Xi views political and economic relations with Russia as a special case requiring a flexible and diplomatic approach. He obviously remembers well how the Russians responded to the Chinese military's incursion into the then-Russian-controlled Damansky (Jin Bao) Island on the Ussuri River in March 1969 which led to the ambush and killing of 60 soldiers of the Russian border force including a colonel, and wounding 94 soldiers on Damansky Island and on the ice of the frozen Ussuri River. In retaliation, the Russian armed forces showered the Chinese border units with Russian long-range artillery shells as well as utilising newly invented, state-of-the-art thermobaric bombs for the first time, wiping out thousands of Chinese soldiers including Mao's 'Red Guards' as well as many Chinese inhabitants of the immediate border region in question, in the process.

The Russian leadership even considered starting an insurrection in Xinjiang similar to the one started in November 1944, which resulted in the creation of the short-lived 'Islamic Republic of East Turkestan' (1945–50), which was liquidated on Stalin's orders after making a deal with Chairman Mao in Moscow.

The Communist leadership of China learned its lesson and refrained from the military pursuit of territorial claims against Russia ever since, signing a final comprehensive border demarcation agreement with Russia on 21 July 2008. Chairman Xi now prefers to attend important Russian celebrations, smile and share a drink with Russian President Putin, sign agreements to build gas and oil export pipelines in Russia's Siberia, and harvest Siberian timber, which benefits China's military-industrial complex by ensuring the uninterrupted supply of oil and gas as well as timber products to the northern regions of China. This benefits President Putin and his cronies of the Russian elite by generating more wealth for them despite depleting vast expanses of the Siberian forests.

This mutually beneficial, cosy economic relationship between Xi's and Putin's regimes culminated in two-way, visa-free travel and working arrangements with Russia prior to the COVID-19 pandemic, benefitting many hardworking and well-educated young Chinese males. Many of these males were then encouraged by the Chinese authorities to subsequently inter-marry local Russian women and settle in Russia, thereby alleviating aberrations of the past one-child policy of China which led to the gender imbalance in China, with a predominance of nearly 30 million young males in China.

The Chinese communist regime has been effectively creating a Chinese 'Fifth Column' in Russia's Siberia and the Far East, with the long-term goal of populating Siberia with ethnic Chinese or half-Chinese citizens and eventually utilising them politically as well as economically to gain control over the region in the future. The COVID-19 pandemic has resulted in the effective closure of the Russian borders, thus disrupting the ongoing trend.

Chairman Xi's main economic as well as military efforts are currently dominated by his strong desire to take full control over the South China Sea and all its natural and marine resources, declaring in the process that the long-established name 'South China Sea' itself, together with its natural and artificially built Chinese islands, is sufficient evidence of them belonging to China, using de facto attempts to establish control over strategically important maritime trading routes. Chinese maps depict Chinese maritime borders near the shorelines or islands of such countries as the Philippines, Brunei, Indonesia, Singapore, Malaysia and Vietnam. All maritime traffic through the South China Sea, where more than one-third of the world's sea freight passes through, is regarded by the Chinese as if it is passing through the Chinese-controlled waterways, and it is only a matter of time before China declares claims to control such maritime traffic as if it was going through Chinese territorial waters.

Chairman Xi Jinping has been expressing through the official Chinese press his clear intention to 'liberate' Taiwan, even if it is likely to lead to a direct military confrontation with the United States as the main ally of Taiwan. Chairman Xi's recent bellicose statements to that effect, declared the need for readiness for war. These comments are clearly made in the hope that firstly, the impressive build-up of the Chinese Navy as well as the Chinese Airforce on the artificially created islands in the South China Sea as well as in the Pacific Region, combined with the massive investments of China in the United States as well as elsewhere in the world including Australia, would preclude the United States from engaging in an all-out military conflict with China on the South China Sea or regarding Taiwan.

President Trump's isolationist views combined with his erratic foreign policies over the last four years of his presidential rule in the United States have given Chairman Xi encouragement to pursue this course of action and possibly even to attempt to 'liberate' Taiwan in the near future, if President Biden proves to be less determined to confront China's aggressive policies in the Asia-Pacific region.

Chairman Xi's China views the South Asia-Pacific Region as vital to its long-term economic and political interests as well as future prosperity. China is therefore determined to dominate the region politically, economically and especially militarily in order to expand its sphere of influence as a global power at the expense of the United States.

President Putin's ill-conceived, criminal 'Special Military Operation' against the free people of Ukraine is not only resulting in the mass destruction of the Russian army and its military assets, but also inflicting untold suffering on the Ukrainian population and wanton destruction on Ukrainian settlements as well as cities. In this regard, Putin has put himself alongside Hitler to be tried by history as a criminal head of Russia to start a war in Europe in the twenty-first century with unpredictable consequences and outcomes.

Xi Jinping, on the other hand, is undoubtedly rubbing his hands in delight, as Russia's defeat and Putin's inevitable demise in this war are likely to enhance China's historical claims against parts of Siberia in the Far East and give China another chance to seize the territory in question from disintegrating Russia, if such a disintegration ends up happening as a result of the war against Ukraine.

Australia as well as all other nations of the Asia-Pacific Region should learn from the tragic fate of the non-Han Chinese minorities of China as well as followers of Falun Gong and draw logical conclusions about what to expect from the communist Chinese regime if and when they fall into the communist Chinese sphere of influence, or end up becoming part of it. Under no circumstances should Australia allow the Papua New Guinea or Solomon Islands leadership to provide open space to China on the doorsteps of Australia to build its de facto military support facilities or bases under the guise of fishing/trading ports or Chinese-controlled settlements, as occasionally mentioned in press releases.

Australia's trade with China should continue and expand on strictly economic terms, as China desperately needs Australian iron ore and other raw materials to fulfil its expansionist ambitions. Therefore, there is no need for the Australian leadership to succumb to political pressure from the Xi regime to tow his line, despite ongoing grovelling noises as well as lobbying efforts to that effect. At the same time, it should be made absolutely clear to Chairman Xi's regime that Australia is fully aware of the ongoing genocide of ethnic minorities in China and condemns such policies perpetrated by Chairman Xi's regime in peacetime. That is why democratic Australia's military and political alliance with the democratic United States must be maintained and strengthened as a permanent part of our long-term foreign policy vis-a-vis Xi's communist clique in China as well as Russia and other countries in the Asia-Pacific region.

It is therefore paramount that Australia's present-day relations with China be confined to economic matters only and at the same time defy and counter all attempts by the Chinese leadership to expand and exert political influence in the Asia-Pacific region. In this regard, the Pacific Islanders especially should be made aware of the tragic fate of ethnic minorities in China as a warning for them of what to expect if they fall under Chinese political and economic control. The Australian leadership should learn how to deal with the Xi regime in reciprocal terms, by slamming export tariffs on strategically important iron ore exports to China and curtailing imports of Chinese consumer goods as a response to the Chinese curtailing imports of coal, wine, barley, meat, lobsters and other valuable foodstuffs from Australia.

The Australian leadership should also understand that Chairman Xi's bullying efforts are part and parcel of his long-term plans to prepare for the invasion of Australia provided that the Americans become weak enough in the future to abstain from an all-out war with China. Australia should build up its defence capabilities by commissioning long-range hypersonic missile systems equipped with thermobaric bombs capable of annihilating the Communist Chinese leadership in Beijing and elsewhere in the event of an all-out war with China instead of its proposed excessively costly submarine fleet, which is unlikely to be as cost-effective and as deadly as hypersonic intercontinental ballistic missiles.

The gradual transformation of Communist China from a quasi-colonial communist country—initially subservient to its Soviet 'older Brother' to the north—into a powerful, modern communist empire with mafia-style, organised communist rule, gradually took place over the last seventy-three years, succeeded with American help in establishing a quasi-market economy controlled by its leadership and incorporating more than 1 billion inhabitants.

The fact that it has been ruled by brutal communist command determined to dominate not only its internal political system, but also the outside world, has been overlooked by western democracies accustomed to fear the Soviet Union and out of that fear accommodating the growth of the Chinese communist regime's economic, as well as military, might.

Chairman Xi's China now plans to overtake the United States both economically as well as militarily in the next ten years and expand its political as well as economic influence through launching Xi's signature trillion-dollar 'Belt and Road' initiative, which is essentially an unbridled attempt to use Chinese money and its economic might to integrate the economies of Asia, Africa and Europe under the leadership and control of the Chinese communist regime, thus challenging American global dominance in economic as well as political and military matters.

As far as internal Chinese politics is concerned, Chairman Xi has proven himself to be a ruthless and brutal dictator and manipulator of public opinion in China, exterminating or assimilating ethnic minorities on the one hand and utilising them as slave labourers after importing them into mainland China factories, and on the other hand accusing followers of Falun Gong and his political rivals of corruption and dispatching them into forced labour camps or the afterlife, while at the same time using controlled state media to depict his image as a 'clean' communist party leader. It is a well-known fact that he is cracking down on overseas Chinese dissidents as well, imprisoning them whenever an opportunity arises as a result of their careless visitations back to China.

These facts do not make Chairman Xi's regime any more humane or less dangerous to the outside world, especially to Putin's Russia with its vast land mass to the north of China as well as abundant natural resources. Russia has so far been oblivious to Chairman Xi's blatant human rights abuses in China as well as the unbridled genocide perpetrated against ethnic and religious minorities, while it is attempting to perpetrate the genocide of its own against the people of free Ukraine.

The emergence of the Coronavirus disease out of the city of Wuhan in the Hubei Province of China should be viewed as the latest manifestation of Chairman Xi's crimes against humanity, as the Coronavirus originated from a bacteriological/viral warfare research laboratory based in that city, which was initially commissioned with the help of French specialists who were given their marching orders after completing their work. The 'Biosafety P4 Lab' has been functioning as a military research laboratory in breach of international conventions prohibiting gain-of-function (GoF) research and development of artificially engineered deadly viruses as bacteriological/viral warfare weapons.

The female scientist, Huang Yanling, conducting gain-of-function research experiments with live bats in that so-called 'Biosafety P4 Lab' containing the largest collection of deadly viruses and bacteria in the world, inadvertently contracted the Coronavirus herself and, after unknowingly leaking it outside of the lab, became one of the initial victims who died in Wuhan on 17 November 2019, alongside many others who died as well in September–November 2019, thus triggering the pandemic initially in the city of Wuhan and its surroundings. The Communist Party leadership first attempted to conceal the dangers posed by the pandemic caused by the gain-of-function research, which produced the deadly COVID-19 virus. The virus then spread from the military 'Biosafety P4 Lab' in Wuhan into the population of the city and its surroundings.

The Xi Jinping regime initially tried to control the situation in Wuhan by gagging and punishing doctors, journalists and scientists who attempted to alert the population of Wuhan and the Chinese leadership to stop the pandemic in its initial stages. When mass casualties started to mount uncontrollably—with a number of doctors and nurses also ending up dead—the Chinese communist leadership was forced to admit the spread of the pandemic and locked down the entire Hubei Province putting close to 60 million people under strict quarantine conditions from 23 January 2020 onwards. By then the Coronavirus was already allowed by Chairman Xi and the

Chinese leadership to spread not only China-wide, but globally. This crime enabled the Chinese leadership to conceal the true origins of the Coronavirus and to claim that it originated from the wet market in Wuhan, despite the obvious fact that such wet markets existed and traded throughout China for hundreds of years without creating any viral or bacteriological pandemics. Criminal attempts by Chairman Xi and his Communist Party leadership to conceal the spread of the newly created, super-contagious Coronavirus, resulted in Lunar New Year festivities proceeding as planned. For instance, more than 40,000 families attended celebrations in the Bai Buting community of Wuhan on 18 January 2020. The Mayor of Wuhan revealed that before the lockdown was announced on 23 January 2020, close to 5 million residents had already left Wuhan to travel all over China as well as overseas, thus leading to the global spread of the pandemic.

The leadership of the World Health Organisation on 14 January 2020 parroted the official Chinese sources in Beijing 'that there was no clear evidence' of human-to-human transmission of the virus, thereby dismally failing to warn the world community of the dangers posed by the unfolding global pandemic and the need to urgently close borders to prevent the global spread of the pandemic out of China.

The COVID-19 death toll in China alone is now conservatively estimated to exceed well over 200,000 persons given that more than that number of extra funeral urns were used in the city of Wuhan alone. On the upper scale of estimates, there is statistical evidence suggesting that there were 21 million fewer cell phone users in China in May–July 2020, compared to the same time the previous year, putting death toll figures attributed to the COVID-19 pandemic in China considerably higher than the claimed 200,000-plus dead victims of the pandemic.

The official twist in the Chinese propaganda machine was the insinuation that the Wuhan Coronavirus 'originated' in the United States and was 'dropped' in Wuhan by a visiting American military sports team in October 2019, prompting the Trump administration to summon the Chinese ambassador to give him an official scolding.

The massive economic and human life losses brought immeasurable suffering to the world community as a result of this major crime by the Communist regime of Xi Jinping. The Xi Jinping clique effectively commissioned the illegal creation of the COVID-19 virus as a mass destruction weapon in the Wuhan 'P-4 Virology Research Institute', which inadvertently escaped from the P-4 Lab and ended up spreading as a global pandemic all over the world. It is now translating into many millions of lives already lost globally as well as trillions of dollars in economic losses. The world community should bring the murderous Xi regime and his henchmen to justice as the criminals who engineered and spread this global pandemic. At the very least, the murderous Xi Jinping regime should be made to foot some of the bills by America and other countries by confiscating all Chinese communist regime assets invested outside of China on a global scale.

The only 'positive' aspect of the Coronavirus pandemic in China under Chairman Xi's rule might be that if all the Chinese communist regime's assets overseas are confiscated to foot some of the global pandemic bills, it might lead to the weakening of Xi Jinping's stance in the Chinese communist hierarchy and may even force him to abandon his attempts to 'liberate' Taiwan in the year 2022 or 2023. He may even be forced to step down as the supreme 'Red Sun' dictator of the murderous Chinese communist regime in the next few years for health reasons or otherwise.

Bibliography

1 Muslimov I B, *Na styke Continentov Yi Tsivilizatsyi*, Nsan Kazan, Russia, 1996

2 Hudiakov M, *Ocherky Po Istoriyi Kazanskogo Hanstva*, Tatarskaya Kniga, USSR, 1991

3 Karimullin A, *Tatarlar*, Tatarskoye Knigoizdatelstvo, USSR 1992

4 A & Z Maski, *Journey To Freedom*, ISBN 0646585304, Ayshe Maski, Adelaide, 2012

5 Ablyazov K A, *Istoricheskaya Sud'ba Tatar, Vol 1 & 2*, Saratov Nauchnaya Kniga, Russia, 2012

6 Enikeev Galy, *Nasledie Tatar*, Algoritm, Moskva, Russia, 2013

7 Rahmanaliev Rustam, *Imperiya Tyurkov*, Gold Medal Einshtein Award USA, Ripol, Russia, 2003

8 Hakimov Rafael, *Istoriya Tatar*, Ruhiyat, Russia, 2002

9 Halikov A K, *Proiskhozhdeniye Tatar Povolzhiya Yi Priuraliya*, Ruhiyat, Russia, 2003

10 Habibullin M, *Soyumbika Hanbika Ham Ivan* Grozniy, Tatarstan Kitap Nashriyate, Russia, 1996

11 Sadri Lailya, *Gomer Yule*, Idel Press, Kazan, Russia, 2003

12 Trofimova T A, *Etnogenez Tatar Srednego Povolzhiya*, Algoritm Moskva, Russia, 2013

13 Leoksin V, Minnikhanov R, *Tatarstan,*Fotoal'bom, Tatkniga, Kazan, Russia, 2011

14 Mukhametshin F H, *Respublica Tatarstan,* Tatkniga Kazan, Russia, 1995

15 Ostrovskaya, A *Strany Vostoka Sin'tzian,* Gosudarstvennoe Economicheaskoye Izdatelstvo, USSR, 1936

16 Sadri Roostam, *The Islamic Republic Of Eastern Turkestan,* Umran Publications, London, 1994

17 Karateev M, *Arabesky Istoriyi,* M Karateev Edicion, Calle, Dorrego, Buenos Aires, Argentina, 1971

18 Murad Adzhy, *Evropa, Tiurky, Velikaya Step,* Mysl, Moskva, Russia, 1998

19 Mustafin M, Huzeev R, *Vseo O Tatarstane,* Tatarskoye Knizhnoe Izdatelstvo, Russia, 1992

20 Gumileov Lev, *Tyseccheletiye Vokrug Kaspiya,* OOO Izdatelstvo, ACT, Russia, 2001

21 Gumileov Lev, *Ot Rusi Do Rossiyi,* Airis Press, Moskva, Russia, 2011

22 Gumilev Lev, *Otkrytie Hazariyi,* Izdatelstvo, ACT, Moskva, Russia 2002

23 Sadri Sagit, *Tatar Bashe Nine Kurmy,* Idel Pressa, Kazan, Russia, 2006

24 *Genocide of Ethnic Minorities in Xinjiang and elsewhere,* various articles, The Epoch Times, USA and Australia 2022.